THE SECOND DAISY

PAT BACKLEY

THE SECOND DAISY

Copyright © 2021 by Pat Backley

All rights reserved.

This book is a work of fiction. Any references to historical events, real people, or real places are used fictitiously. Other names, characters, places, and events are products of the author's imagination and any resemblance to actual events, places, or persons, living or dead, is entirely coincidental.

All rights reserved. No part of this publication may be reproduced, distributed, or transmitted in any form or by any means, including photocopying, recording, or other electronic or mechanical methods, without the prior written permission of the publisher, except in the case of brief quotations embodied in critical reviews and certain other commercial uses permitted by copyright law.

Pat Backley
www.patbackley.com

Paperback: ISBN: 978-0-473-59905-8
ebook: ISBN: 978-0-473-59906-5
Kindle ISBN: 978-0-473-59907-2
Audiobook ISBN: 978-0-473-59908-9

Edited by Colleen Ward.

Cover design by 100 Covers.com
Formatting by Formattedbooks.com

CONTENTS

Acknowledgements v
Chapter 1 **1985, Artillery Passage, Spitalfields London** 1
Chapter 2 **1985, Marylebone, London** 11
Chapter 3 **1985, Montague Mansions, London** 21
Chapter 4 **1991, London** 29
Chapter 5 **1992, London** 43
Chapter 6 **Starting Again** 57
Chapter 7 **New Beginnings** 71
Chapter 8 **The Big Adventure** 99
Chapter 9 **The Journey** 107
Chapter 10 **New York, New York** 125
Chapter 11 **Alabama** 139
Chapter 12 **Farewell to Harlem** 147
Chapter 13 **Return to England** 155
Chapter 14 **The Next Chapter** 161
Chapter 15 **An Unexpected Thing** 171
References 189
Author Biography 191

ACKNOWLEDGEMENTS

This book is dedicated to my beloved daughter, Lucy. I would also like to thank everyone who has inspired me to write this sequel.

It has been wonderful to revive some of the characters from my first novel, *DAISY,* bringing them to life again to tell this story.

So much of the inspiration for my writing comes from people I know closely, people I have met somewhere along my journey, and people who have touched my soul.

Thank you all.

1985, ARTILLERY PASSAGE, SPITALFIELDS LONDON

Daisy had always loved looking at old family photographs.

When she was a little girl, she used to get so excited every time Great-Grandma Flo got out *The Box*.

They called it a box, but actually it was an old metal tin.

Black, oval shaped, and rather battered.

It was crammed full of old photos of her family—of people she had heard about, but had never known. When she was young, Daisy would often snuggle up next to Flo on the squashy old brown leather sofa in the kitchen, the two spending hours poring over the old memories.

Daisy loved the house where her great-grandparents lived, in Artillery Passage in Spitalfields.

The solid brick building, more than 200 years old, was enormous, with five floors, a courtyard garden, and a huge cellar. They had lived there since they were first married in the 1920s, so the house was full of stories about the lives they led.

The ground floor was Daisy's favourite because she could walk from the narrow cobbled alleyway straight into the shop.

Great-Grandma Flo's shop was called "POLLY'S," and when Daisy was little, she had thought it was named after her mum and Flo's granddaughter, Polly.

However, Flo had explained to the little girl that she had actually named the shop after her own grandma, Polly, who had died in 1890, more than a hundred years ago!

Daisy had always wished she could have known *that* Polly, mother of the original Daisy, her namesake.

She loved hearing all the family stories and was disappointed that there were so few photos of the two of them.

In fact, there were only two photos of the first Polly. They were small faded sepia pictures that you had to screw your eyes up to see clearly. But even though they weren't very clear, you could still tell that Polly had been beautiful, with long, blonde, curly hair and a pretty smile.

There was one photo of Polly and her little girl, the first Daisy, sitting in a park. The little girl was wearing a necklace and a bracelet made from small daisy flowers. The second picture was a formal pose, obviously taken in a photographer's studio. In that one, a young man called Fred, looking very smart and obviously in his best Sunday suit, stood behind two women: Polly and someone called Sybil, and little Daisy.

Daisy had grown up hearing so much about these people, her ancestors and extended family. She wished she could have met them. But of course they were all long dead now.

Her Great-Grandma Flo, Great-Grandad Joe, and Grandma Vi had lived in the house in Artillery Passage forever. It was where her mum, Polly, and her Aunty Penny had grown up.

Apart from Daisy's own home, the Mews Cottage in Marylebone, where she lived with her mum and dad Jeremy, as well as her Nana and Grandpa's home in Brixton, Artillery Passage was the place she loved most in the world.

Actually, that wasn't true. She also really loved the mansion in Bloomsbury where Aunty Melissa, Aunty Ruth, and Matty lived.

They were all very old now of course, almost ancient. So it was lovely to get the old photos out and see how they all used to look when they were young.

"Oh love, do we really have to do this again?"

Flo groaned and pulled a face, but Daisy knew she didn't really mind. Her great-grandma loved looking at all the old photos as much as she did.

Daisy loved her tall and cuddly GG Flo so much.

She had decided to call her GG when she was quite small, finding "Great-Grandma Flo" too much of a mouthful.

Somehow the name had stuck, and now, even though she was a big girl—aged fourteen—she still used the affectionate term.

To her, GG seemed so ordinary, just like any other great-grandma. It was hard to believe that she was one of the most famous dress designers in London and had been since the 1930s. Everyone knew the label, *Polly's*, but very few people ever realised that Flo was the woman behind it. She was so modest, never seeking praise and always shying away from any kind of publicity. She had always loved designing and making beautiful clothes, clothes that any woman would be delighted to wear, and she was much happier out of the spotlight, quietly sitting in her little shop still sewing beautiful dresses completely by hand.

The only thing Flo flaunted was her original creation, the very first dress she had ever designed and made. She had discovered her passion for sewing when she was just fourteen years old, still a schoolgirl with absolutely no idea what she should do with her life other than become a good wife and mother. One day, she came across an old trunk belonging to her mum. It was crammed full of beautiful fabrics. She had been so inspired; she knew immediately that she had found her passion. In just a few days she had sewn a stunning gown for herself. When she eventually opened her dress shop, she had hung this first dress in the window. There it remained until this day, a constant vision of beauty, a muddle of colours, stitched lengthwise so the pieces of fabric hung like petals.

"GG Flo?"

"Yes, my love?"

"Why do you keep that old dress hanging in the shop window? It looks a bit old and tatty up there, next to all the lovely new ones you make."

"Oh Daisy, when you are older, you'll understand. Sometimes the things in life that are the most precious aren't the things that are brand new or cost a lot of money. Sometimes it's the little things, the things that bring you memories, that matter more."

"Oh, okay."

Flo knew by the way the little girl spoke that she really didn't understand at all. To Daisy that old dress was just that, an old dress. But to Flo it meant everything. It had been the start of her passion, something she could call her very own. Something that no one could ever take away from her. That first dress reminded her of so many people she had loved and lost: her mum Daisy, and dad Blackie, Sybil, and young Fred, and of course, Old Frederick Palmer, the millionaire. How she missed them all.

It also made her think of when she met her Joe, and how she married him on a snowy Christmas Eve when she was just 18 years old. Sometimes she felt a bit sorry for him; his life had turned out so differently from what he had expected.

He had wanted to live south of the river, near his family in Southwark. Then she had found this place in Spitalfields, perfect for her dream of opening a dress shop. He had "given in" to her wishes, but she knew how happy he was, how happy they had both been during their long and loving marriage. Neither of them ever had any regrets.

"I suppose you girls want a cup of tea and some ginger cake while you're doing that?"

Daisy's Great-Grandad Joe chuckled as he spoke. He made the best ginger cake in the world.
Even her Nana Winifred said that. Mind you, her Nana Winifred in Brixton made the very best fried chicken in the whole wide world!

And so, while Joe bustled around the kitchen making cups of tea and slicing big chunks of ginger cake, they began.

Although Daisy had looked at them so many times before, she never tired of it. After all, these people were her family, her ancestors, the people who brought her into existence.
When she was little, she often remarked on the colours. Not the colours of the old sepia photos, the faded black and white shots, or the more recent colour prints, but the colours of her ancestor's skin.
In the earlier days, even up to the early 1970s, most of the people in the pictures had white skin. Now, all the family photos were different. Black and White, Black and White, all happy and posing together.

Daisy had never really thought about the colour of her skin until she went to school.

She was used to her own family. Dad, Nanny, Grandpop, Uncle Matty, and Aunty Ruth were all Black, and Daisy's mum, grandparents, great-grandparents, Melissa, and all the others in her family were White. Daisy herself had skin of the most glorious shade of coffee, golden and rich.

"GG Flo, please tell me again about how it all started."

Flo cleared her throat and took a deep breath before she began.

She held the first photo and her voice shook a little as she spoke. It didn't matter how many times she told the story, it still made her cry.

"It all began in the Workhouse, back in Victorian times.

Your great-great-great-grandma Polly was born there. We don't know anything about *her* mum, except that she was young, beautiful, and a great seamstress. She died giving birth to Polly. Times were very hard back then."

Daisy knew this was true. They had been learning about the "olden times" in her history lessons at school and she had been horrified to learn about the poverty and cruelty that so many people endured.

"When Polly was just eleven, she was sent out to work. They had discovered that she was quite good at sewing just like her mum, so they sent her into service at a big mansion near Regent's Park."

When Daisy was small, Flo used to skim over the next bit, trying to protect the child from the awful truth. Now that she was almost a young woman, however, it was better to be honest.

"That's where she met Fred and Sybil. They both worked in the big house too and they took Polly under their wings. Sadly, the master of the house mistreated her and she ended up giving birth to Daisy, my mum."

Flo paused for a moment. This bit always made her cry.

"Unfortunately that brute wouldn't leave Polly alone, and she died giving birth to another of his babies. She was only 19 years old."

"GG Flo, you told me before that Polly doesn't have a proper gravestone, that she was buried in a pauper's grave. What does that mean?"

Flo continued to tell her sad tale. How Daisy, her mum, had lived in the slums before being looked after by Old Frederick.
The family history was rich and varied; Daisy was enthralled as always.
As Flo told each chapter they fished out the relevant photographs, and for several hours they were lost in the mists of time.

"So, did *your* life turn out how you planned?"

The young girl stared intently at her great grandmother as she spoke.

"Oh Joe, that girl is a funny wee one. She has such a big heart. If you'd seen the way she wept when I told her about Polly and Daisy... and she wants to know everything, every last detail about the family history."

Joe just smiled. How he loved seeing those two together, his magnificent wife and their great granddaughter, Daisy. The little girl who had stolen all their hearts.

1985, MARYLEBONE, LONDON

Jeremy heard the call pulling into the Mews and quickly put away his tape measure.

"Hello, my gorgeous girls."

Polly looked over at her handsome husband and smiled. She still found him incredibly attractive. Somehow he seemed to have become even more handsome over the years, and the sound of his deep, velvety voice still gave her butterflies.

Daisy had already leapt out of the car and rushed into his arms. She loved her father passionately.

"Did you have a good time with GG Flo?"

"Oh yes Dad, it was wonderful. We had tea and ginger cake and looked at all the old photos. And we made a design for a dress for my school ball. GG says her eyes aren't good enough to sew anymore, but she said that Mum can make it for me. She said that *she* made enough dresses whenever Mum wanted them as a young girl, and that *now* it's Mum's turn to make them for me!"

Jeremy and Polly exchanged a grin.

"GG is quite right, my love. She did make heaps of dresses for me, and although I'll never be as good as her, I don't do a bad job at keeping the old shop going."

Since Flo's eyesight had started to fail and her arthritis had made it difficult to sew properly, she had been taking a back seat in the shop.

Determined not to let it close, which would have broken her heart, Flo had persuaded her granddaughter, Polly, to keep it going. Polly opened the shop on Tuesdays, Thursdays, Saturdays, and by appointment.

Polly had always been a capable (though reluctant) dressmaker, but Flo was still the brains behind the outfit, keeping the accounts and planning all the designs.

Daisy was very happy that her mum worked, it meant that after school and during the holidays, she would always take Daisy back to Artillery Passage to be looked after by Flo and Joe, while she was busy in the shop.

Most Saturdays while Polly was working, Daisy would go down to Brixton with her dad Jeremy to visit her other grandparents, Samuel and Winifred. She loved them dearly and would often beg to be allowed to sleepover so she could go to church with them on Sunday mornings. She just adored the little gospel church in Brixton, the singing, and the music. She was very proud when Grandad Sam would, on occasion, play his saxophone during the service. And of course, everyone at the church loved her, this beautiful little girl with the coffee-coloured skin, sunny nature, and big heart.

Jeremy and Polly didn't mind at all when little Daisy begged for a sleepover at her grandparents' house, as it meant they could have a rare, romantic night alone together.

They were still madly in love. The tall, handsome Black man and his almost as tall, beautiful White wife. They had been married for 15 years now, but sadly Daisy was their only child. They had desperately wanted more, but after three traumatic miscarriages, it seemed it would never happen. Over time, they had come to terms with the sadness. At least they had been lucky enough to have one healthy child, and what a joy she was.

Their little Daisy was the light of all their lives. Her sunny, optimistic nature ensured that any time spent in her company lifted their spirits. She was bright, beautiful, and intelligent, and Jeremy had high hopes of her joining the family business one day.

Not Polly's, the dress shop in Artillery Passage, but the small architectural firm he had started a few years ago, after he had finally qualified as an architect.

It had been a long road, a really hard slog, and one that he had often thought about giving up once he had a wife and child to support.

But Polly had never let him give up on his dream. *She* was the one who kept all the balls in the air, ensuring he always had good meals to keep his energy levels up, as well as a quiet place to study.

To keep them afloat financially, Polly had willingly taken on various odd jobs to support the family: working as an office assistant at the local school, selling Avon cosmetics door to door, typing letters for a grumpy old solicitor in his dingy office on the High Street, and even joining her mother-in-law Winifred and her office cleaning team for a few months.

Jeremy realised how lucky he was to have such a fine wife; hardly a day went by when he didn't tell her how much he loved her. He remembered when he was a little boy and had planned to find a wife as nice as his mum—he had certainly managed that!

Of course, it had helped enormously that they had never had to worry about getting a mortgage or paying rent. They lived in the Mews Cottage, the house that Polly's family had given her as a wedding present. It was the same cottage that Old Frederick Palmer, the millionaire, had given to the first Daisy on the day she married Blackie the coalman, back in 1905.

Jeremy looked around the room, planning things in his head.

"Why are you looking around like that? Why have you got that funny expression on your face?"

He had never been able to hide anything from her. She always said that he would make a rotten poker player, that every emotion showed on his face.

"Oh I was just thinking about something."
"What?"
"Nothing really important."

Daisy was eavesdropping from the other room. She had rushed in there to turn on the television. Tonight was Top of the Pops night and she didn't want to miss it. All the girls at school would be discussing it tomorrow.

"Jeremy, why did you hide your tape measure when we came in? What are you planning now?"

Daisy listened through the open door.
She could always tell that when her dad went quiet, he was up to something. Usually it was something nice, a treat for her and her mum. He was such a good, kind person, and even though he was getting a bit old, he was still quite good looking. In fact, lots of her friends at school had a crush on him.

Jeremy was now in his mid-thirties, and although his daughter thought he was ancient, he was actually still in the prime of his life.

He blushed, and although it was a little hard to see on his handsome black face, Polly knew the signs.

"Come on, tell me. Otherwise, I'll phone your mum and tell her not to make fried chicken for you on Saturday!"

He laughed. She knew his weaknesses; she knew him so well. She knew that his mum's fried chicken was his favourite food in the world. It held so many good memories for him, not just the delicious taste, but the sheer comfort of it. He suddenly had a flashback to when he was 11 years old and starting at the grammar school. He had been bullied mercilessly there, just because of the colour of his skin. And always, when he came home in tears, his mum would be there, with a steaming plate of her delicious fried chicken.

"Okay, okay, I'll tell you."
Polly laughed.
"Oh Jeremy, you are so easy to wind up. As if *I* could stop your mum from making your very favorite meal!"

Polly loved her in-laws, Winifred and Samuel.
She couldn't possibly have asked for better ones. They showed exactly the right amount of love, support, respect, and caring. They never interfered, but were always there if needed. They fitted so well into her family; it had been a seamless process to intertwine the lives of her Brixton in-laws with that of her Spitalfields and Bloomsbury relatives. It was a source of constant joy to her, to see just how close they had all become. And of course, everyone came together to adore their little Daisy.

"Well," he spoke hesitantly, unsure of how she would respond.
"I was wondering if perhaps we could divide off a bit of this room and turn it into an office for the business. The rent is going up on that poky little place I rent on the High Street and I thought, as we have so much room here…"
His voice dwindled.

"I think that's a great idea, love. I don't know why you didn't think of it before."

So, while Daisy was engrossed watching Madonna cavorting across the television belting out her new hit song "Like a Virgin," her parents were measuring the room next door, planning where to put doorways, windows, and electric sockets.

"You need to have three proper desks. One for you, one for your dad, and one for a secretary. And lots of filing cabinets for all your records. And nice blinds at the windows. And a proper wooden front door with a brass nameplate."

Jeremy smiled to himself. He loved this woman so much. This was *his* dream, not hers, but she was so supportive, so lovely.

"I think Dad is going to be thrilled with this new plan. Shall I phone him now and tell him?"

Polly went into the kitchen to make dinner while Jeremy was on the phone. She could hear the excitement in his voice.

"Hi Dad, it's me. Sorry to ring a bit late, but I just wanted to give you some news. Polly and I have decided we want to make an office here at the Mews, rather than continue to pay rent for that crappy little room on the High Street."

"Yeah, we've just measured it all out and there's plenty of room. Room for you, me, and a cute little secretary!"

Samuel, standing in the lounge of the house in Brixton, put down the phone and slumped into a chair. His wife, Winifred, looked across and spoke gently.
"Is everything alright at the Mews, love?"

"Oh sorry, Win. I expect you'd like to have chatted to our boy too. Sorry, he just took the wind out of my sails a bit. They've decided to move the office to the Mews. Sensible plan. It's silly to pay rent and make someone else rich."

She waited. He looked a bit shell shocked; there must be more to come.

"He says he wants me to work there full time, as a partner. With my name on the door and everything."

Winifred heard the catch in his voice, and, perching on the edge of his chair, hugged him tightly.

He didn't say anything else for a while and she knew his mind was whirring.

He and Jeremy had always been very close, and the boy knew everything about his father. His hopes and plans, his thwarted dreams.

When Samuel had been a young man growing up on the mean streets of Harlem in the 1930s and 1940s, he had dreamt of becoming an architect. However, that wasn't possible for a boy like him, a boy descended from slaves.

Instead, he got a job as a cleaner at Minton's Playhouse. That's how he had met *her*, Winifred, the love of his life.

They had moved to London when Jeremy was just five years old.

It had been a difficult transition for them all, not quite the glorious, gold-spangled future they had hoped for. It had been hard to settle, hard to get a decent home or job, and they had been shocked at the racial prejudice. It was something they thought they had left back in America. Jeremy had been so badly bullied at school, just because of the colour of his skin.

Eventually though, they were happily settled.

In Brixton, at first in a rented flat, then in a little three-bedroomed 1930s semi-detached house. They had saved hard to get the deposit, but once Jeremy had finished studying and left home, his parents seemed to have a bit of spare money. Therefore, they had taken out a mortgage with the Abbey National Building Society. In a few years, it should all be paid off.

The only job Samuel had been able to get in London was working as a bus conductor for London Transport. After 30 years he had grown to love the job, although he only did a couple of shifts a week nowadays, just covering for sick leave and holidays.

"So will you give up the buses now, Sam?"

"I guess I'll have to, Win, if I'm going to be a partner in a posh architect's firm."

She could hear the pride in his voice. Pride, and excitement too. At last, he was going to fulfill his long-held dream, a dream he had never expected to reach. She sent up a silent prayer of thanks, to God and to her beloved son, Jeremy, for making his father so happy.

"Jeremy says he's going to change the name of the firm, too."

At the moment, the firm was called "JP Architects," named after Jeremy and Polly.

"He says it will be 'JPSD Architects' now."

"Oh Sam," Winifred hugged him tightly, both of them close to tears.

"And I suppose the D is for Daisy?"

Jeremy was hoping that when she left school, Daisy would choose a career in architecture. She was certainly smart enough and had always loved drawing, but time would tell. At least her initials would already be on the nameplate.

1985, MONTAGUE MANSIONS, LONDON

The mansion, *The Home for Retired Gentlemen,* in Marylebone, was a splendid place.

Established more than 40 years earlier by Mr. Frederick Palmer, it was a wonderful final home for single men, men who had never married because they preferred the company of other men.

Frederick Palmer had been such a man himself.

Disinherited by his own father because of his sexual preferences, he had, in later life, enjoyed a long and loving celibate friendship with another Fred. They were two men from entirely different backgrounds, but they developed a deep and affectionate bond.

Frederick had decided, before he died, to turn his mansion into a place where like-minded men could spend their final years being looked after in a loving and caring environment. He wanted the house to be somewhere they could relax, somewhere they would not be judged. It was a very happy place.

He had ensured that there was a large enough sum of money left in his will to enable the mansion to run for at least 60 years.

Old Frederick had often been heard to say that he "hoped, by then, by the year 2000—the turn of the next century—that the world would be a kinder place, more understanding of the fact that not everyone wanted the same thing, that not everyone wanted a wife and child."

Daisy was sitting upright in one of the mahogany chairs from the library. She would have much preferred to be curled up on one of the old leather sofas, but this was a Wednesday afternoon and it was her day to read to the residents. Today, she had chosen *The Old Curiosity Shop* by Charles Dickens.

Daisy paused in her reading and looked around the room.

There was old Mr. Price, who was only pretending to listen; she could see his eyes fluttering and desperate to close. Then there was Mr. Johnson, sitting upright with his silver-rimmed glasses perched on the end of his large nose.

Mr. Webb, in his bright, red waistcoat, yellow shirt, and brown trousers, was staring at her intently as she read. His hearing was getting pretty bad but he was too vain to wear hearing aids, so he tried to lip read.

Gerald Fox sat with all the other old codgers—as they liked to refer to themselves—in the spacious lounge at Montague Mansion.

A few of them were nodding off in their armchairs, a couple were even snoring rather loudly, but all his attention was on the little girl.

Mr. Fox was yet another snappy dresser, like old Mr. Webb.

Before he had come to reside at the mansion, Gerald had lived alone for many years in a little basement flat in Belgravia. Well, it was not really a flat, but more like a studio with a bathroom. He had been living there all alone since he first arrived in London as a naïve and troubled young man. He had left his home village in Suffolk as soon as he could, having been stifled there—bullied mercilessly by the other kids at school because he was gentle, quietly spoken, and more interested in art and design than in football and fighting.

It had been such a relief for Gerald to arrive in London, a place where nobody knew him, a place where he could just be himself without sticking out like a sore thumb. He had never quite plucked up the courage to make many friends and certainly had never had a lover, but he found his niche working as a window dresser in one of the large department stores in the West End. There, his talent and rather flamboyant tastes proved to be great assets for his success. It was at the store in Piccadilly that he had met Old Frederick Palmer. The rich, aristocratic man often stopped in to chat and admire the window displays Gerald had created, and, once recognising a kindred spirit, had invited him and the other window dressers from the store to a Christmas soirée in Marylebone. Over the years they had become good friends: he, Mr. Palmer, and young Fred. They shared many interests with one another: a love of art and design, good books, the theatre, and of course, stylish and fashionable clothing. They also all knew how it felt to stand out and endure difficult situations just because they didn't conform to the normally-accepted standards of society. Gerald had adored the evenings he spent with the two older men. He enjoyed the cosy suppers and long evenings relaxing in front of the roaring coal fire in the mansion's library, nursing crystal tumblers of the best whisky and brandy. After those wonderful evenings, he always hated going back to his lonely, cold, and rather damp basement flat.

Gerald fell into a routine for life, and had never dreamt that much of anything would ever change. Therefore, it came as a surprise to him when, a few years later, Frederick Palmer announced his intention to turn his mansion into a home for retired gentlemen. Gerald was invited to be one of the first residents and at that, he felt as though he had died and gone to Heaven. He moved in more than 40 years ago and every day spent in the mansion was the happiest day of his life. It had come with such great sadness when both the old men, his benefactors, had died of old age. However, because of their foresight and generosity, he and all the other residents of the mansion were still living a life of relative luxury.

Today, Gerald was wearing his pale-blue silk shirt and pink trousers with a pale-pink cashmere sweater draped over his shoulders. He looked around the room, irritated to see his fellow residents not paying attention to Daisy's reading.

"Daisy my darling, pray continue. I regret that some of these chaps are just heathens; their reading ability probably doesn't stretch much beyond the daily papers. I doubt they were ever as bookish as you and I."

The girl smiled at him and continued to read:

> *"They came upon a straggling neighbourhood, where the mean houses parcelled off into rooms, and windows patched with rags and paper, told of the populous poverty that sheltered there. The shops sold goods that only poverty could buy, and sellers and buyers were pinched and griped alike. Here were poor streets where faded gentility essayed with scanty space and shipwrecked means to make its last feeble stand, but tax gatherer and creditor came there as elsewhere, and the poverty that yet faintly struggled was hardly less squalid and manifest than that which had long ago submitted and given up the game."*

By the time Daisy had finished reading the chapter, all the old chaps were nodding in their chairs, even Mr. Fox.

Daisy had been reading to them since she was a little girl. Even before she could truly read properly, she had insisted on climbing up onto one of the antique mahogany chairs and pretending to read from her picture books.

Of course, the old men adored her from the start. To many of them, she represented the child they never had—the child they had never been able to have because of the people they loved.

The mansion was a splendid place and of course, because she lived right next door in the Mews Cottage, Daisy could pop over whenever she liked.

She loved it. It was like having a whole house full of grandfathers.

Daisy loved to hear the stories from GG Flo about the mansion, about all the family history.

How the millionaire Frederick Palmer had fallen in love with young Fred the footman, and how Sybil and the then—young Daisy—the first Daisy—had been taken under Frederick's wing.

The first Daisy's bedroom, next to the basement kitchen, was still intact. It was a large room full of silk, satin, and treasures, all untouched for many, many years. The space was kept as a shrine, almost. It was not a sad and creepy place, but a place that shone.

Daisy would often go into the room, sit on the brass bed, and think about her ancestor—the first Daisy.

GG Flo was a wonderful source of information about many things, and Daisy cherished their conversations.

Luckily, although GG Flo was pretty old, she still had all her marbles; she could still remember most things and she and Daisy would often sit on that brass bed and talk about those who had gone before them.

THE SECOND DAISY

Flo would often get very emotional as she talked about her parents—Daisy and Blackie.

Like this young Daisy, Flo had also lived in the Mews Cottage until she married her Joe, just after her 18th birthday, back in 1924. Old Frederick Palmer had given the cottage to her mum as a wedding present. He had taken care of Flo's mum, Daisy, the little girl from the slums, since she was 14 years old. Once she was married, Frederick still had wanted her to stay close by, so that he could continue attending to her—and later to her daughter's—every need.

What a fine gentleman he had been; their family owed him such a debt of gratitude.

Frederick had been the one who had bought the house in Artillery Passage for Flo, back when she was newly married and announced that she wanted to open a dress shop.

So much history, so many unique connections that brought everyone together.

1991, LONDON

Sometimes, Daisy thought the last six years had gone by in such a flash that they almost seemed like a dream. She was now almost 21 years old, but in some ways it seemed no time at all had passed since she was just 14 and had spent long, happy afternoons reading to the old chaps at the mansion house.

How she had loved them all. She smiled as she thought about old Gerald Fox and his love for rather outrageous clothing. He had often said that in another life, he was quite sure he must have been Beau Brummell, the Regency dandy.

Mr. Fox was still alive, but he was now a mere shadow of his former self.

He slept most of the time, nodding off in his armchair every day after lunch. However, he always perked up on a Wednesday afternoon when Daisy popped in to read to the men.

Despite everything else that had gone wrong in her life, going into the mansion to read was still one of her greatest joys and she tried very hard to never miss a week. After all these years, Daisy had read from nearly every book in Frederick's well-stocked library. Still, the classics—Dickens, Austen, and of course, Oscar Wilde—were their very favourites.

In the last few years, it hadn't been very easy for Daisy to keep up these Wednesday rituals. Sometimes, she had to sneak out of the house without mentioning where it was she was going. *He* had been so very jealous.

But now, *he* was out of the picture. Thank goodness.

It had all started so well.
She had been just 17 when she met him, the tall, dark, and very handsome man. He was the stuff of a teenage girl's dreams.

"Mum, can I bring a friend home to lunch on Sunday?"

Polly smiled and looked up from the book she was reading, *The Pillars of the Earth* by Ken Follett.
It was one of Jeremy's favourite books. As an architect himself, he loved the story of the medieval cathedral builders. Polly had been reluctant to start it as it was such an enormous book. It was much too heavy to balance easily in her small hands, but after a few pages she was totally engrossed, lost in the world of Kingsbridge and its inhabitants.

"Yes of course love. Who do you want to bring?"

Daisy had always been a very sociable girl. Even when she was very young she had loved making new friends and inviting them home. The little Mews Cottage was often bursting at the seams.

"His name is Henry. I met him at college. He lives in Wimbledon."

Daisy had, for the last six months, been attending Kingston Polytechnic College. She knew that her mum and dad were disappointed that she had decided not to stay on at school and then apply for a place at university.

She was a bright girl and easily able to achieve the grades needed, but somehow, despite her bravado and confident manner, she was rather shy and unsure of her own abilities. Perhaps that was why she enjoyed reading so much. It was a way of escaping into a different world, a world where she could imagine herself as a heroine, performing all sorts of glorious, wonderful deeds.

"Of course you can bring him love, what would you like me to cook?"

Daisy smiled wryly.

She knew that nowadays, her dad did all the cooking at home. *He* would be the one who prepared something delicious on Sunday, not her mum.

She loved both her parents dearly and knew how incredibly lucky she was to have them. They were always there and always supportive of her, whatever she did and however much of a mess she made of her life.

When she was a teenager, Daisy had gone through a few years of not liking them much. They had seemed so boring, so restrictive, never wanting her to go out and have fun. Her dad insisted on driving her everywhere, to parties or even just to friend's houses, and somehow he always seemed to linger long enough to check that there were responsible adults around to supervise them.

She had been embarrassed by him, and by the fact that some of her friends seemed to have a crush on her dad. Her *dad,* a man old enough to be their father. She had to admit though, he didn't seem quite as ancient as some of the other dads. One of her friends even thought he looked like Sidney Poitier, the actor. She didn't really know why—maybe just because he was tall, spoke beautifully, and had black skin.

Anyway, Henry had come to lunch that Sunday and had coped very well with meeting Daisy's family.

Her mum had insisted on inviting everyone, the whole extended family. It was so embarrassing—almost like an interrogation.

There had been her mum and dad of course, as well as Grandma Vi, GG Flo, and Great-Grandpa Joe from Artillery Passage.

"I really think we should invite Melissa, Matty, and Ruth too, and of course Sam and Winifred. We haven't all been together for ages!"

Daisy knew her mum just wanted them there as backup, the rest of their loving, extended family.

She hadn't thought to mention to Henry that half her family was Black. She had just assumed he would realise that because of the colour of her own skin.

However, he had looked a bit surprised when he was introduced to everyone and had obviously struggled to work out how they all fit into the family tree.

It was obvious that Daisy's parents explained her own dark, coffee-coloured skin.

Then, it was easy enough to work out that one set of grandparents—Sam and Winifred—were obviously her dad's parents, and that Vi, Flo, and Joe were from her mum's side. However, he looked puzzled when he was introduced to Melissa, Matty, and Ruth.

Melissa was still incredibly elegant at the age of 88. Her looks belied her age and in many ways she still acted like a young woman. She was White and spoke with a deep, Southern accent. She had been born in Alabama, the daughter of a wealthy cotton plantation owner.

Matty and Ruth, Melissa's friends and long-time companions who were now in their late nineties, were Black. They were from Alabama too, and had both descended from slaves. For almost seventy years, the three of them had lived together at Bedford Court Mansions in Bloomsbury.

Daisy often thought that her family was like history come to life.

There were tales of slavery, poverty, and hardship, as well as riches and adventure.

Her grandparents, Samuel and Winifred, descended from slaves too.

They had come to England as a young couple with her dad when he was only five years old, leaving behind their life in Harlem.

The little family had been hoping for a glorious, gold-paved new life in London, but instead they had been shocked to find themselves shunned, treated rather badly, because of the colour of their skin.

Looking back, Daisy realised she should have noticed the warning signs in Henry.

The red flags.

At the time though, Henry had seemed so charming. It appeared that he was delighted to blend in with her rather exotic and unusual family.

"I'm not so sure about that lad. Somehow, I don't think he's as genuine as he wants our Daisy to believe."

"Oh Joe. Please don't say that. Our Daisy is obviously in love with him and I'm sure he's truly a nice lad."

Flo, Joe, and Vi were all back at the house in Artillery Passage following the lunch at the Mews.

Vi, Daisy's grandma, rarely said much. Usually she either had her head in a book or was busy doing her shop window displays; she had worked for many years at some of the biggest and best department stores in the West End.

So, on the odd occasions when she did have something to say, they always stopped and listened.

"Well, I think Dad might be right. He's a bit too cocky for my taste. Reminds me of some of the rich young twits we get in the store, full of their own self-importance. Too much money and not many brains."

A similar conversation was taking place in Bloomsbury.

"Oh dear, I really hope our Daisy isn't making a big mistake. That young man is just a bit too full of himself for my liking."

"I agree, Melissa. Considering it was the first time he had met any of us, he seemed mighty familiar, too arrogant for such a young man."

Both women looked across at Matty, where he was slumped comfortably in his favourite old leather armchair.

The still-handsome old Black man smiled at them before he spoke. How he loved them both and always had, ever since they left Alabama all those years ago. Back then, they had only left for a small holiday, a much-needed break from their grief and sorrow at losing Matty's best friend Theo, Melissa's one and only husband. She had been widowed after just one year of wedded bliss. They hadn't even had enough time to make a baby. The three of them mourned him still.

Matty's glance lingered on Ruth then, his wife.

She was aging so well, so gracefully. Men still stared at her as she walked down the street. He remembered the night he first realised he was in love with her, an evening back in the 20s when they had all gone to the jazz club on Wardour Street. Ruth had been wearing a pink dress, it was flapper style and of course, all the men had wanted to dance with her.

The beautiful, intelligent Black woman, descended from slaves, had stolen all their hearts.

Out of all the men in the club that night, Matty was the one who had been lucky enough to marry her.

Sadly there had been no children, but nevertheless, they had had a wonderful life together. They, as well as Melissa, had lived life to the fullest, a happy little threesome who had travelled the world and found adventures together.

Matty cleared his throat before he spoke. Now that he was getting on a bit, he sometimes found his voice wasn't quite as strong as it used to be.

Turning ninety-nine earlier that year had come as a bit of a shock.

In his head, he was still a handsome, sexy young man, playing his saxophone in the nightclubs and being admired by all the young women. It was pretty hard to accept that nowadays, he was invisible to just about anyone under the age of 30, just another decrepit old man.

"I know what you mean, Melissa. He certainly was very full of himself. A rather privileged, self-important young man. Reminded me a lot of some of the young folk we used to know back in Alabama. Never did a day's honest work in their lives, just living off their daddy's money."

"Oh, like me you mean, Matty?"

The three of them burst into laughter.

It was true that Melissa had grown up with a silver spoon in her mouth, but the way she had since lived her life had proved how different from her upbringing she really was.

When they had stopped laughing, Matty spoke again.

"I am worried. Our girl seems very besotted and he is certainly the wrong one for her. But of course, whatever we say, she will make her own mistakes. At least when it goes wrong, we will all be here to pick up the pieces."

Months later over at the Mews Cottage, in the offices of JPSD Architects, Jeremy and his father Sam were poring over plans for a new extension to a trendy dress shop on the High Street.

"Dad, do you think it's too late to talk sense into her? Every time I bring up the subject, she flies off the handle and stalks off."

"Oh son, our girl has a mind of her own. You and Polly have seen to that. But I know what you mean. I'm really worried too, and so is your mum."

The only one who had no reservations about the upcoming wedding was Daisy herself. At the age of 18, she knew everything.

"Oh Mum, I don't know why you and Dad are making such a fuss. I love Henry and he loves me. All of the women in this family have gotten married young and, apart from Grandma Vi, everyone stayed happily married forever."

It was true.
The first Daisy had married Blackie the coalman when she was just 18.

Great Grandma Flo married at 18 too, and her Grandma Vi had only been 17 when she *had* to get married. Even her Aunty Melissa had only been 19 when she married Theo, the love of her life.

And so it was done.
Against all the wishes and advice of her family.
It was a big, glorious white wedding in a beautiful old stone church with hundreds of guests, pale pink roses and lily-of-the-valley filling every available space.

Daisy had looked magnificent in a stunningly beautiful white satin gown. She had six little bridesmaids in pale pink dresses, trailing behind as she walked up the aisle on the arm of her handsome father, Jeremy.
He didn't look as proud and happy as the father of the bride should.
Instead, he looked rather anxious, unsure whether he was leading his beloved daughter, his only and much-loved child, towards a life of joy and happiness or one of misery and sorrow.

Polly sat quietly in the front pew, wedged between Vi and Flo, looking at them constantly and hoping someone would be brave enough to stand up and stop the proceedings.
But of course, no-one did.
Daisy would never have forgiven them. She was determined to enjoy her day, the day she was a real princess wearing the beautiful gown that her great grandma, her mum, and Aunty Ruth had worked so hard on. Even her mum's sister,

Aunty Penny, had done a few stitches on it. She had surprised them all by returning from India, where she had lived for so many years, for the wedding.

The groom, Henry, looked a little worse for wear.

He had been out the night before on his stag do, with all his mates from college and a few old-school chums. By all accounts it had been a fairly riotous night; they were all looking a bit grey this morning. Even the smart morning dress and pink rose buttonhole he was wearing did nothing to disguise his white, rather sickly-looking complexion. Polly just hoped her new son-in-law did not embarrass them all by being sick into his top hat!

Eventually, the event came to an end.

The bride and groom bade fond farewells to their guests and went off to spend their wedding night in the honeymoon suite before flying out to Paris the next day.

Henry's side of the family had just departed on their way back to Wimbledon, leaving a trail of confetti, whisky fumes, and expensive perfume in their wake.

"Did you see the way his mother looked at our Daisy? Like she wasn't good enough for her precious boy!"

Flo spoke angrily.

Daisy was *their* family treasure, far too good for the likes of that stuck-up Henry and his lot.

Flo had tried to engage Henry's mother in conversation at the wedding reception, but when she mentioned that she lived in East London and ran a dress shop, that wretched woman had turned her head to speak to someone else, someone she considered more suitable to *her* social standing.

That stupid, snooty woman obviously had no idea that she, Flo, was the award-winning proprietor of one of the most exclusive and sought-after dress shops in the whole of London.

Melissa spoke quietly, but they could all hear the anger in her voice.

"That despicable woman sums up everything I hate. She thinks that because they have a big house in Wimbledon, drive a smart car, have a cleaning lady, and take holidays abroad, they are somehow better than the rest of us.

And did you see the way they looked at Ruth and Matty and Samuel and Winifred? They even managed to look down their stupid new money noses at our Jeremy."

None of them had ever seen Melissa quite so angry.

She was especially angry that despite ignoring the Black members of their family and talking down to the White ones like Flo, Joe, and Vi, who all lived in the East End, Henry's snooty mother and his other relatives had been eager to talk to her, Melissa, the rich American heiress.

Still, at least that awful day was over now, and hopefully none of them would have to encounter Henry's horrible family until there was a christening!

1992, LONDON

Three years later and it was all done.
  Over.
  Finished.
Divorced.

Daisy often looked back on her wedding day and wept.

She wept for the naïve, innocent girl she had been. A girl so trusting, so unquestioning, and so utterly sure of her own mind.

Big mistake.

Thank God she'd had her loving family to fall back on, to pick her up when she had crumbled into a million disappointed, heartbroken pieces.

They never once said "I told you so," they had just been utterly supportive and understanding.

She knew it had broken all their hearts to see her suffering, but they never interfered. They just tried to let her sort it out for herself.

It had all started to go wrong a couple of days after their big, smart, and expensive wedding.

She had been so happy. A new bride on the arm of her handsome husband, strolling down the streets of Paris.

They had stopped outside the Moulin Rouge nightclub in the Montmartre district.

Henry had been very keen to buy tickets for that night's show, but she was hesitant, unsure whether she wanted to share her new husband with all the scantily-dressed performing women. Instead, she was happy to just take a couple of photos of the outside of the club, to capture the image of the big windmill and the bright lights that spelt out "MOULIN ROUGE."

"You will never fit all that into one photo. Don't even bother trying."

"Oh, that doesn't matter Henry, I just want to prove I was here."

She had barely finished speaking when he grabbed her camera. It was a little Kodak Brownie that her dad had bought her especially for their Paris trip.

"It's a nice, easy little camera for you to carry and use, my love. Don't forget to take lots of pictures of all the lovely buildings for your granddad and me to study—just in case we never get to Paris ourselves!"

She had been so shocked when Henry snatched the little camera out of her hands and threw it on the pavement. Then he started shaking her, holding onto her shoulders tightly so she couldn't escape. Eventually he let her go, but only after he realised onlookers were staring, wondering what on earth this pretty little girl had done wrong to be treated so badly in such a public place.

In the blink of an eye he had straightened up, picked up her smashed and broken camera from the pavement, and, taking her arm, firmly steered her away from the watching crowd.

Afterwards, she wondered if she had imagined it.

Had she just imagined that Henry suddenly turned from a loving, attentive new husband into a kind of monster, into someone she barely recognised?

The rest of the week passed quickly with only a couple other slightly worrying incidents. Henry got very angry when a local Parisian sent them to the wrong metro station, and also when a waiter at the cute little bistro near their hotel in the Madeline district served them the wrong bottle of red wine.

Henry considered himself to be something of a "wine buff," and was most annoyed that "a mere Frenchman should think he knows better than me, an English gentleman, what vintage Côtes du Rhône to choose."

Daisy never mentioned these incidents to anyone.

It had been so embarrassing and certainly not something she wanted to share with the rest of the world, especially her family.

She knew they would all be horrified and judge him harshly, even though he had already explained to her in a very calm and patient manner that it wasn't *his* fault, sometimes he just had these moments of anger. He said they always passed quickly and were nothing for her to worry about, unless *she* was the cause of his anger. So, could *she* please ensure that she was always a good wife, and never do anything to instigate such moments?

Daisy was just 18 years old. She was naïve, loving, and endlessly trusting. She had never seen such raw anger before, and it frightened her. But, she had willingly married this man against the wishes of her loving family. She had to make the best of it.

For two years she had tried desperately to make the best of it.
She tried to pander to his every whim.

She had given up her college course because he said he wanted her at home to keep their new little flat in Roehampton spick and span and ensure that he had a hot meal on the table every night.

He had left college at the same time as her to work for his uncle's estate agency in Wimbledon, selling houses to the rich and famous.

Of course Daisy had wanted to stay on at college, to finish her course on English literature from the 19th and 20th centuries, but he was adamant.

He wanted her to stay at home and after all, as he said, she could easily read all the books she wanted then.

The real reason he wanted her home was because he was jealous.

He had seen how popular his beautiful young wife was amongst all their fellow students and he wanted her out of the way, tucked safely away in Roehampton. There, her charm would go unnoticed.

She had tried so hard to be a good wife, the kind of wife he obviously wanted. She tried to be the wife who would happily stay at home all day, clean his house, wash and iron his clothes, and prepare his meals. She never raised her voice or questioned his decisions. In fact, she soon realised that he would much rather her not have any opinions at all, about anything.

Daisy began to wilt.

She felt herself getting smaller and more insignificant as the months, then years, ticked by. She missed the fun and camaraderie of college. She missed the impulsive pub lunches and strolling around the town between lectures with her friends.

In fact, she missed her friends terribly. She had always been such a sociable girl, but now it seemed that her friends had all drifted away, off to a life of which she knew nothing. A life full of fun, laughter, and music, of parties, pubs, and weekend outings to the seaside. This was a life that Henry would not allow her to have.

She tried to fill her time with other things. She tried out every new recipe she could lay her hands on, producing delicious meals served beautifully on bone china plates she had inherited from GG Flo. They were pretty plates with gold hand-painted edges and sprigs of orange and yellow flowers in the centre. She always ensured that her and Henry's tatty little Formica kitchen table was covered in a clean, starched white cloth, that the house was clean, the laundry washed, the entire space in order.

She soon realised that she was wasting her time, that none of it mattered to Henry. Her cooking didn't please him at all; apparently it didn't measure up to the fine cuisine his mother had always served him. There was either too much salt or not enough. Too much onion or not enough cheese. The potatoes were too hard or not crispy enough. The meat should have been cooked for at least another half an hour.

When she was feeling rebellious, Daisy sometimes stood up to him—if she felt the criticisms were particularly unfair. However, she soon learnt that that wasn't wise.

When Henry got angry, his neck started to go very red and his shoulders tensed. By now Daisy had learnt to read the signs, but because she was an intelligent, feisty girl she sometimes went too far. Then, she was lost.

He would get up from the table, pushing his plate to the floor. He would shout at her, telling her what a stupid, selfish little bitch she was and how he wished he had never married her. Then he would stomp off to the bedroom, slamming the kitchen door behind him so hard that it made the glass panes in the windows rattle. If she was lucky he didn't always hit her, sometimes he just yelled, but occasionally, she would have to stay indoors for a few days afterwards so that no-one would notice the bruises.

Once when they had been married for about a year, it had been particularly bad and she'd had to stay home for a whole week. She hadn't even been able to go to the mansion that Wednesday afternoon to read to the old boys; they would certainly have noticed the bruises on her neck from where he had put his big hands, threatening to squeeze the life out of her. Not to mention, her mum and dad would definitely have intervened if they knew how badly he was treating her.

So, she told no-one. She just tried to endure it all on her own. She tried to convince herself that if *she* just tried a bit harder, it would be fine. They would get back to the happy early days, the days when he had seemed to adore her before becoming her husband.

Sometimes Henry was charming, usually only when other people were around. Then, he acted like the perfect gentleman—the perfect husband.

Daisy shuddered as she remembered the day of the curtains. She bought some beautiful floral material at the market. It was white linen fabric covered in yellow and orange daisy-like flowers, to match the dinner plates. She bought enough to make curtains for the little kitchen and dining area, as well as a couple of cushions and some table napkins. She had been so excited at the thought of brightening up the rather cold and dreary room.

She didn't have a sewing machine and had never really been interested in sewing, but it was a good distraction, maybe even the start of a new hobby. The windows were not very large, so it wouldn't take her long to make an attempt at sewing them by hand.

"I don't know why you're bothering with that, Daisy. My mum offered to give us some of the old curtains from her guest room."

"Oh Henry, I just thought it would be nice to make some myself, to make the flat more homey."

"And you think that cheap muck from the market is going to do that, do you?"

"Well, I was just trying to save money. You must admit, it is really pretty fabric, lovely bright colours, and my grandma says they sell the same stuff in the big department stores, just at four times the price."

She was sitting on the floor with the length of fabric spread out in front of her, holding the steel tape measure she had borrowed from GG Flo's dress shop. She had already marked, with a piece of tailor's chalk, the lengths for each curtain. Although she wasn't naturally gifted at sewing, she was a perfectionist and had spent enough years watching the other women in her family make things to know how to do it. On the floor next to her was a pair of big, heavy brass scissors, just perfect for the job.

She was so engrossed in her project that she didn't notice him rise from the armchair where he had been lounging, watching her as she worked.

Suddenly, he grabbed hold of the heavy scissors and threw them at her, barely missing her face. She cowered as he stood over her, his face getting redder and redder as his temper rose.

"You are just so stupid, Daisy. You don't even know how to cut out a piece of cheap material properly. You might as well just throw it all in the bin right now. I can't bear to watch you. I'm going to the pub. Don't bother to make me any dinner."

She never told her family any of that. If she had, she knew they would have arrived in Roehampton, probably the whole lot of them at once, and rescued her. It was her pride that stopped her. She knew they had all been against the marriage in the first place. She didn't mind admitting when she had made a mistake, but she had only been married for such a little while, and maybe Henry was right when he said she should make more of an effort. She really should just try a bit harder to stop provoking him.

Henry thrived in his new role as an estate agent.

His good looks and youth combined with his charming, rather effusive, and slightly flirtatious manner, appealed greatly to the ladies of Wimbledon.

He worked long hours, often not getting home until 9 or 10 at night, by which time he seemed to only be interested in a glass of whisky and his bed.

He hardly ever bothered to ask Daisy how her day had been, and certainly showed no interest in her nor in the delicious dinners she had prepared for him, dinners that then dried up and festered in the oven.

Poor Daisy. She really didn't know what to do. She was sad, lonely, miserable, and far too ashamed to tell her family about any of it.

And of course, because she tried so hard to be a good, obedient wife rather than standing up to him for fear of provoking his anger, everything only got worse.

Occasionally, Henry didn't bother to come home at all.

He would just ring and say that a client had insisted on taking him out to dinner, then ring again around midnight to say he was too drunk to drive home, so was staying at his uncle's house.

This went on for two years before Daisy finally accepted the truth.

Two long years.

She had gone to the agency Christmas party.

Henry hadn't wanted her to be invited, but his uncle said it would look odd if the newest partner to the firm did not have his wife there.

She felt very out of place.

Her skin colour had always set her slightly apart from Henry's family.

She had often overheard loud whisperings, questions about her background and origins. She knew that some of his older relatives were rather unhappy he had married a "coloured girl."

The party was held in a smart restaurant in Wimbledon.

They had taken over the whole place for the evening and decorated it with Christmas baubles and tinsel, in rather garish shades of orange and lime green—the agency colours.

On every spare table there were piles of brochures, printed in the same hideous shades of lime and orange, boasting about the company's successes in selling houses worth over one million pounds. She noticed that Henry's beaming face was featured on several of these, proclaiming him as "Agent of the Month."

This had seemed very odd to Daisy.

Whenever she asked him for money to do the grocery shopping, he always grumbled, saying she must learn to economise, not be so wasteful, that money didn't grow on trees and he only earnt a pittance.

Yet, here he was, clearly popular and successful. Even she knew that estate agents earnt commission every time they sold a house.

It was quite a miserable evening for Daisy who stood mostly on the sidelines, trying to play the dutiful wife whilst watching Henry being feted and flirting with some of the clients as well as a few of his female colleagues.

Once the party was over and they were back at the flat in Roehampton, she dared to start a conversation. "Henry, you are obviously doing all right at work. Do you think I could get a little part time job? It's quite boring being home all day on my own, and you work such long hours that I hardly see you. The library is advertising for a part-time assistant."

Daisy spent an interminable number of hours at the local library. It was her only solace, apart from when she visited her family or sneaked out for her reading sessions with the old boys at the mansion. Occasionally her family came to the flat in Roehampton, but that made her uneasy. Henry never seemed happy to have visitors, even if he wasn't home.

He had been undressing and turned to face her. She wished he would just take her in his arms, make her feel special.

"Oh God, Daisy. What are you moaning about now? You embarrassed me tonight, standing there like a miserable, old sourpuss, hardly cracking a smile. And that dress you were wearing really didn't suit you; it made you look a bit old and frumpy."

She didn't stop to think of the consequences before she answered.

"Oh, and I suppose I was meant to look happy while you ignored me all evening so that you could flirt with all those women? It was truly quite embarrassing watching you grope that little tart with the fake tan and false boobs. And don't think I haven't noticed that lipstick on your collar."

He looked down at the shirt he had discarded on the floor. She was right, there was a lipstick stain on it. Bright red, the colour that Heidi, the new office girl, wore faithfully.

"I noticed the same colour lipstick on your shirt last week, and tonight I recognised her by the smell of her perfume. It's the same perfume I have smelt on your clothes every night for the last two weeks."

Henry was silent for a moment, then he grabbed her by the hair and pushed her against the wall. She could smell the alcohol on his breath as he snarled at her.

"At least I have a bit of fun with her. She laughs at my jokes and thinks I'm witty and sexy. You've changed, Daisy. You aren't the girl I married anymore."

He let go of her hair in such a rough manner that she felt the pain in her scalp, then he threw her to the floor.

"I'm off to bed. Wake me up at 7.30; I have an appointment with a client at 9 in Brixton."

Daisy sat up until four in the morning, alternating between drinking cups of strong black coffee and weeping.

The next morning she woke him at 7.30 as requested, and he left the house at 8.45 without giving her so much as a smile, let alone a kiss.

Then, she packed two suitcases.

She left the flat keys and her wedding ring on the kitchen table, and caught the number 74 bus home to Marylebone—home to the Mews Cottage—and the safe, comforting arms of her mum and dad.

STARTING AGAIN

Being home was like being curled up in a big, soft, feather eiderdown.

Her mum and dad said nothing when she turned up, exhausted from lugging the two heavy suitcases all the way from the bus stop. They simply hugged her tightly and put the kettle on.

Her grandad Samuel was there too, working in the office, and he just gave her one of his big lopsided smiles and said, "Welcome home, my darling."

The first few days were a blur.

Henry kept phoning, demanding that she go home—back to the cold, uninviting flat in Roehampton. He never talked about love, just kept repeating that she was *his* wife, as if all that mattered was that she was his possession.

In the end, after he had made her cry for the umpteenth time by telling her how selfish she was being, she began to waver, thinking that perhaps she should go back to him and try to make a go of it once more.

She hadn't realised that her parents were eavesdropping on her calls, but suddenly the phone was snatched from her trembling hand.

She had never heard her dad sound so angry before. Her mouth opened in shock and her mum, who had come to sit beside her on the sofa, squeezed her hand gently.

"Okay, Henry." Jeremy's deep voice trembled with rage.
"This is quite enough. You'd better stop ringing Daisy.
No, you may not speak to your wife. In fact, she won't be your wife for much longer; you will be hearing from our solicitor very shortly. I suggest you count yourself lucky that I am a reasonable man; I know of no father who would feel content with the way you have treated my daughter. I am truly sorry that she ever laid eyes on you."

With that, Jeremy thumped the phone back onto the receiver and looked like he was about to cry.

"Oh, Dad."

Daisy had never seen him look so upset before. Her dad was always so happy, loving his life and his little family.

She got up to hug him, but her grandad beat her to it.
"There, there son. It's okay. You have done a fine thing, standing up for your girl like that. I am very proud of you."
Samuel remembered the last time he had seen Jeremy so upset.

It had been more than 30 years ago, when he had started at the grammar school and had been racially targeted and beaten every day for months.

Somehow, seeing how much Henry had upset her dad strengthened Daisy's resolve.
Anyone who could hurt her lovely dad like that was not a real man, certainly not someone she would ever want to spend the rest of her life with.
And so it was over.

That very day they got in touch with Polly's Uncle John, whose partner Nigel ran a legal firm in Nottingham. They got him to begin divorce proceedings immediately.

Uncle John, Grandma Vi's brother, had always been on the fringes of the family.
Loved, but never quite understood.
He had been a quiet boy who had left home as a young man to go to university and become an engineer. Instead of returning to London after he qualified, he had chosen to stay in Nottingham, and although he came back every Christmas and for special family occasions, he never talked much about his life.
Great-Grandpa Joe and Grandma Vi had always known he was gay, but it took a long time for GG Flo to come to terms with it.
It had been illegal to be homosexual for so many years and it had never truly been accepted, especially since the AIDS epidemic.

So, in an effort to protect his family, John had kept his life in London and his life in Nottingham far apart from one another.

However, as he started to get older, and especially since his parents had grown old, John had surprised them all last Christmas by bringing his long-term partner, Nigel, to Artillery Passage with him.

Of course, they had all got on like a house on fire; John's family had been warm and welcoming, just sorry it had taken so many years for them to meet Nigel, the love of John's life.

Since then there had been lots of visits, so Jeremy had no qualms about asking for Nigel's help in getting Daisy out of her disastrous marriage.

The divorce was granted quite quickly on the grounds of Henry's behaviour.

He was very angry and said he was going to contest it initially, making Daisy wait until they had been separated for two years for it to be finalized.

It was an agonising time.

Divorce is never easy, and the loving family who watched helplessly for two years as they saw their girl go from being a vibrant young woman to an anxious, pale shadow of her former self, just wanted it all to be over.

Their dream was for it to be finished, so that their lovely Daisy could get on with her life.

The turning point finally came when her solicitor wrote to Henry, saying that Daisy was willing to give up her share of the Roehampton property in exchange for her freedom.

The flat had gone up considerably in value since they had bought it, so Henry could see himself making a good profit on it. At the same time, he was already involved with Heidi, the girl from the office. In fact, she was now five months pregnant, so it would be good if he could make an honest woman of her before their baby was born. Not to mention, his family thought she was much more suitable than Daisy had ever been.

It was heartbreaking for Daisy's family to watch her suffer. They could see how devastated she was that her marriage had failed. It seemed that there was nothing any of them could say that would make it any better.

"I think I might take Daisy out for lunch on Saturday and try to get her to talk a bit."

Grandma Vi was probably the only one who really understood what she was going through. She was the only other person in their family to have been divorced. She too had suffered because of a cheating husband, a husband who had eventually abandoned her for another woman, another life.

The Hotel Café Royal on Regent Street in London was a splendid place.

For more than 100 years it had been the place to see and be seen, frequented by the likes of Oscar Wilde, Winston

Churchill, Noel Coward, Mick Jagger, Muhammad Ali, and Diana, Princess of Wales.

Daisy knew the restaurant well; it had always been a favourite place for family celebrations. They had been coming here every birthday and anniversary for as long as she could remember.

"Do you remember the first time your dad ordered the steak and stilton, just because he had read somewhere that it was what Winston Churchill always ate when he dined here?"

Daisy laughed, suddenly getting an image in her head of her lovely dad trying to emulate the great statesman.

"And the time that Melissa insisted we all try oysters, but Flo and Joe refused because they said that when they were young, only poor people ate oysters!"

"I remember the first time Aunty Melissa brought me here for afternoon tea.
I think I was only 7 or 8 years old and I was so excited. She said it was very important that I experienced it for the first time on my own, without any of you here to distract me! I couldn't believe how beautiful the place was, all these vast rooms with high ceilings and fancy furniture. I thought it looked just like a palace and I pretended I was a real princess. We had cucumber sandwiches with the crusts cut off, and fancy little cakes with pink and violet icing."

For the first time in months, Daisy was quite animated as she spoke and Vi smiled quietly to herself. It looked as though her plan was working, the plan to distract Daisy from her misery and bring her back to life in a gentle way.

"I am so glad I never came here with Henry," Daisy said, a bit tearful.

"If I had, I don't think I would have wanted to come today. In fact, it would have really spoilt it for me if I had memories of *him* in this lovely place.
I hate going places that he and I went to together. Somehow, they all seem a bit tainted."

Vi replied quickly, desperate to lighten the tone and distract Daisy from such gloomy thoughts.

"Oh, my love, you never have to go anywhere with *him* again. That miserable bit of your life is over now. Thank God you were brave enough to leave him when you did—before you had a couple of kids."

She realised she had said the wrong thing when she saw the tears welling in her granddaughter's eyes.

"Oh Daisy, I'm sorry. I didn't mean to make you cry. Don't you worry, one day you will find another man—a good one this time—and then you can have all the babies you want."

"How did you cope, Grandma, when your husband cheated on you? You must have felt so bad when he went off with that other woman."

It was well-known in the family, the sad story of Vi's short, disastrous marriage.

Everyone knew how she got pregnant when she was 17, just as she was starting out in life. She thought that she was in love with Bert, the docker from Southwark. Now, she knew that it had just been infatuation, that she had been flattered by him, flattered that he had chosen her over some of the older, prettier girls he usually hung around. And of course, he had reminded her of her father. Joe, who was also a docker, was a different kind of man altogether. He was a wonderful man—kind, gentle, and utterly loyal. Still in love with her mother even after all these years.

"Sometimes it all seems like a distant, bad dream; one day your current troubles will feel like that, too. At the time I thought I just wanted to die, to give up on life altogether. I had just given birth to your Aunty Penny. I was only 17, much too young to have a baby and I had no idea how to be a mother. I didn't want to be one at all really, but in those days there was no choice. If you got in the family way before you were married, you put shame on your family. Some poor young girls were thrown out of their homes, left to fend for themselves and their babies on the streets. I was truly lucky that my mum and dad helped me. They were really disappointed in me, but they never let me down. I was lucky too, that Bert agreed to marry me. His family wasn't too pleased; they thought I was a bit snooty because I worked up West in a big department store. On top of that, I refused to move to Southwark after the wedding. Good job I didn't go, the way things turned out."

She paused and took a big gulp of tea from the fine bone china teacup in front of her.

Daisy was stunned. She had never heard Grandma Vi talk so much. She was usually the quietest one in the family and here she was, telling what seemed to Daisy like her whole life story. A story so personal and raw that Daisy thought she might burst into tears.

"I had very bad baby blues after your Aunty Penny was born. For months I couldn't seem to shake off the blackness. I cried almost all the time, couldn't be bothered to get out of bed most days, hardly combed my hair or got out of my pajamas sometimes. Everyone was a bit worried about me, worried that I was losing my mind. In those days it was considered a weakness, an affliction, something to be spoken of in hushed tones. Now they just call it postnatal depression."

Daisy leant across the table and stroked her grandma's hand. It was the first time in her whole life that she had ever really thought about her grandma being a young woman, a frightened girl forced to deal with a situation that she was much too inexperienced to handle.

"Were you ill for long, Grandma?"

Vi wiped away a couple of tears that were rolling down her face.

"Oh my love, it seemed like forever to me at the time. It was like I had fallen into this big, dark hole, and although I tried really hard, I just couldn't climb out of it. Then one day, about a year after I had the baby, Bert left. He just went away and never came back. From that moment on I began to get better. I think it was because I could relax. I didn't have to try to be the perfect wife or perfect mother. I could just go back to being me, to being Vi."

"What happened after he left? I heard he had another woman."

"Yes, that's right. He had obviously been carrying on with her for quite a while, because she was already pregnant when he left us."

"So, did you have my mum when he was still around?"

No-one had told Daisy much about her mum's birth.

"A few months after Bert had gone, I realised I was pregnant again. It was such a shock and I knew everyone was worried it would just tip me over the edge. But your mum's birth was the best thing that ever happened to me. She was a real shining light at the end of a very dark tunnel. Polly was such a beautiful, happy, easy baby. She hardly ever cried, not like your Aunty Penny who cried all the time. Your mum's arrival was the turning point. She gave me a new reason to live, a purpose. I tried to love my two girls equally, but I guess I've always had a real soft spot for your mum."

"Is that why Aunty Penny ran away to India when she was so young?"

Vi laughed, but Daisy could see the pain in her eyes.

"Oh, Daisy. I don't like saying it. It makes me feel like such a rotten mother, but yes, it might have been one of the reasons. She always said she just wanted to have an adventure, but I think maybe I did make her feel second best in some way. I will always feel guilty about that."

Daisy remembered how happy she had been to see Aunty Penny at her wedding, her mum's rather mysterious and elusive older sister.

The last time she had seen her was a few years before the wedding, when all the women of the family had taken a trip to India.

It had been a crazy, colourful, marvellous visit, a time of joy and reconciliation. It was a time of mending a few broken bridges, bridges that had never been intentionally broken but were broken nonetheless.

It had been wonderful for Daisy to see her mum laughing and joking with Aunty Penny. They were very similar physically, both tall and rather beautiful, but poles apart in their personalities. Penny was much quieter and seemingly content to be a fly on the wall; if it hadn't been for the bright vibrant colours of her saris, she would have just blended into the background.

Daisy's mum was the complete opposite. She was much louder, more confident, and more outspoken. However, they were both kind and loving. Neither of them could pass a beggar on the streets of Mumbai without foraging in their purses for a few spare coins.

"We had a wonderful holiday when we all went to India, Grandma. We had such fun and it must have been lovely for you to spend time with both your girls."

Vi smiled. This girl was just like her mother. Her Polly wouldn't hurt a fly, all she wanted to do was make everyone around her happy. She beamed at her granddaughter and took another bite of her cucumber sandwich. How could such an ordinary thing as a cucumber sandwich taste so utterly delicious? It just had to be the glorious surroundings that made it taste so good.

The afternoon drifted on pleasantly. The two talked non-stop, which was extremely unusual for Vi, but somehow, in Daisy's company she was more relaxed, more able to talk about her feelings, even those feelings she had been bottling up for years.

As they left the restaurant, Daisy linked arms with her grandma and kissed her lightly on the cheek.

"This has been a great afternoon. Thank you so much, Grandma. I don't think I've ever heard you talk so much before. I wish you always would, you have so many interesting things to say. I haven't thought about Henry all afternoon."

The afternoon tea with Vi had helped her to perk up a little, but Daisy was still far from the bright-eyed, eternally happy girl she had once been.

She tried so hard to drag herself out of her misery. She just felt like such a failure. Everyone in her family had such happy marriages, marriages that lasted forever. How could she have been so foolish, so trusting, and naïve? How could she have believed that marriage to a selfish man like Henry would be the answer?

Since hearing Grandma Vi's story Daisy had felt a bit better, a bit less of a mess. Vi had helped her realise that her future happiness was up to her, not to some random Prince Charming who may or may not appear in her life. No, her future was firmly in her own hands. At least she knew she always had the loving support of all her family.

NEW BEGINNINGS

"Daisy my love, why don't you come down to Hastings with us tomorrow?" asked Jeremy. Samuel looked up from the set of plans he was studying.

"That's a great idea, son. Yes, I think you should come with us, Daisy. We could really do with some help and you have a great eye for detail. Besides, there are a lot of handsome young men working on the site, and they would probably love to see a pretty girl like you. It would make their day."

Daisy poked her grandad with the metal ruler she was holding.
"Ouch, that hurt!"
"Don't be so dramatic, Grandad, it hardly touched you!"

"What on earth is going on in here? This is supposed to be an office, not a children's playground!"

They all turned to look at Polly, who was standing in the doorway with a tray of steaming hot mugs full of coffee alongside a china plate piled high with freshly baked cheese scones.

"Oh Mum, those look good. Have you put in plenty of butter?"

"Stop trying to change the subject, my girl. You know I always spread lots of butter on them. More to the point, why are you poking your poor grandad with a ruler?"

Sam clutched his arm theatrically and pretended to moan in pain.

Daisy laughed.
"Oh Mum, you know how dramatic Grandad is. I didn't even hurt him!"

"Good. You should always treat people as you would like to be treated, and I am quite sure that if he did it to you, you would scream the place down!"

They all laughed and settled down at their desks to eat the delicious scones and drink the coffee. It was exactly eleven o'clock on a cold and rainy London morning, just the right time for such a treat.

"What time are you setting off for Hastings tomorrow, Jeremy?"

Polly smiled at her husband as she spoke.

Jeremy was the love of her life. How it warmed her heart to see these three people working together: her husband, his father, and her beloved daughter.

It had always been Jeremy's dream that one day, Daisy would join the family firm of JPSD architects. He had initially set up the firm after he qualified, hoping one day he could pass it onto his children. As it turns out, Daisy was the only child he and Polly had been able to have. They had lost three babies, all late miscarriages, and now that they were both in their early forties it looked as though Daisy would always be their only one. Now, they didn't care. She had brought such joy to their lives over the years; she had made their marriage complete. These days, they just wanted to make her happy, to bring back the sparkle that Henry had taken away from her.

"I think we'll drive down quite early, Poll. We want to avoid the traffic, so probably we'll go about 10. That way, we'll be there in time for lunch. I wish you were coming with us, then it would be like a little holiday. But I know you're busy at the shop."

"Oh Jeremy, I wish I could come, but it's so hectic at the shop at the moment. We have a big order for some fancy Knightsbridge wedding. The bride is lovely; she already adores the dress Flo designed for her. The only problem is that her mother is a nightmare. She is constantly changing her mind. One minute she wants to look like a typical mother of the bride in pastel florals, the next she thinks a Spanish flamenco look might be better. We are all tearing our hair out. I think Flo would have chucked her out of the shop if we hadn't all liked her daughter so much."

"So what is GG Flo going to do? Is she going to tell her to get lost? I think she should."

They all laughed. Daisy was so protective of her great-grandma. Woe betide anyone who upset Flo when *she* was around.

"I think Flo has come up with a solution. Last night she showed me a design that kind of incorporated both looks. She is so clever. It makes total sense how she's managed to be so successful in business for all these years. She is just so good at coming up with great designs. I don't know how she does it, how on earth she thinks of all these things."

It was true. Flo designed her first dress when she was just 15 years old. And now, 70 years later, she was still designing dresses that women wanted to wear—even difficult, almost impossible-to-please women.

"Never mind, love. Perhaps we can all go for a few days next month. I know Win is keen to spend some time down there too. She just loves foraging around in all those antique shops in the Old Town—buying more rubbish to fill up the house! I think she's taking a few days off soon, so perhaps we can all book something then."

Sam was not aware that every time he mentioned his wife's name, he smiled a slow, lazy smile that lit up his eyes. In his eyes she was still the same fabulous, feisty woman he had met in Harlem all those years ago.

"Anyway Daisy, are you going to come with us or not?"
Sam turned his head to look at his beloved granddaughter.
"Oh Granddad, I don't know. I don't think I'd be of much use, just hanging around holding tape measures while you and dad do all the work. But I do like the Royal Victoria."

The Royal Victoria Hotel, on the seafront in Hastings, was a great favourite with all the family. They had first gone there when Daisy was just five years old for a little weekend break. It had proved to be the perfect escape, just an hour's drive from London.

In the end, with a little persuasion from her mum, Daisy decided to join the men for their outing the next day. They arrived in Hastings in time for lunch and as always, Daisy was enthralled by the old hotel. Built directly opposite a big shingle beach, the magnificent building erected more than a hundred years before, had always reminded her of a palace, a smaller version of the Queen's home in London. She loved the grand, rather old-fashioned atmosphere, the marble pillars, the high ceilings with their decorative cornices, the afternoon tea, and the slightly faded exquisiteness of it all.

After lunch, they wandered up to the site on Warrior Square.

Warrior Square and the hotel were actually situated in St. Leonards, rather than in Hastings itself. There was apparently a clear disembarkation between the two, with the inhabitants of St. Leonards considering themselves a cut above their Hastings cousins—unless you lived in the actual Old Town area of Hastings, then you were also considered part of that cut.

Warrior Square was a magnificent place. Built in the mid 1800s, the enormous square of large houses had often been described as "Belgravia by Sea."

It was set amongst large manicured gardens overlooking the seafront, fronted by an enormous bronze statue of Queen Victoria, which had been erected in 1902.

When she was a little girl, Daisy loved strolling around these gardens, running up and down the paths, and stopping to admire the pretty flowers. She had been especially enthralled by the stories Great-Grandad Joe told her, of how he had visited Hastings as a little boy, on the old steam train. He had pointed out the bullet hole in the skirt of Victoria's statue and had made Daisy laugh by telling the story of how it got there during an air raid in WW2. Her GG Joe was such a mine of information; it had always seemed to her that he knew everything about everything.

She had always loved Hastings.

Lots of people said it was boring, faded, a typical English seaside town past its best, a place whose glory days were long behind it.

THE SECOND DAISY

Over the years, some of the big houses in Warrior Square had gone through many changes. They had gone from being affluent, sought-after establishments to sometimes shabby, unloved squats. However, they always retained their classic bones, the remaining notes of other, grander times.

Jeremy and Samuel had been given a brief to renovate one of these such gems: a once-beautiful period home that had since fallen into disrepair. Originally a hotel, a place of grand proportions and exquisite fittings, this space had sadly become a rundown former shadow of its glorious self. It was now a place that was threatened with demolition, thought to be beyond redemption—a rabbit warren of little rooms with all the original architectural features boarded over and forgotten about over the years.

On their first visit a couple of months earlier, Jeremy and Sam had gingerly peeled back rotting plasterboard and were amazed to find most of the original features still intact. Magnificent ornate plaster cornices, marble columns, and original oak staircases were all buried under the ravages of 1960s and 1970s modernisation.

They had been selected for the job by an acquaintance of Melissa's in Bloomsbury. She had been living there, in Bedford Court Mansions, since the 1920s, and was something of a local legend. Everyone knew the old American lady—the heiress from Alabama—who lived there with her two Black friends, Matty and Ruth.

It had taken many years, decades even, before they were properly accepted by some of the older tenants of the mansion block, but as time passed and the old brigade died out, the mansion flats were sold to smart young professionals, people who were glad to have such a fun, eclectic group in their midst. Many of these new people dabbled in business, often protected from the cut and thrust of real enterprise by family money. Melissa understood them. She too had been protected all her life by her daddy's money.

A few of them became property developers and over the years, persuaded by tumblers of her best gin, they began to try out the services of JPSD Architects. She had been amused to see their faces when Jeremy and Sam turned up for the initial meetings. She rather enjoyed watching the discomfort on her neighbours' faces when they realised that the people she had recommended for the job were Black. This is because, of course, their reticence had completely dissipated over time, blown away by the sheer expertise and professionalism they saw from the two men. *They* then began recommending JPSD to all their friends and colleagues, and in just a few short years Jeremy and Sam had almost more work than they could handle. It was good, solid work too, work that would and did earn them a great reputation. Melissa was thrilled. All her life she had tried to fight inequality—particularly inequality borne of racism—and now, without bloodshed, she felt that at last she was making a difference. Leaving a legacy of which her beloved husband Theo would have been proud.

The young tradesmen working on the Warrior Square site were delighted to see Daisy. In fact, a few of their mouths dropped open and one man almost fell off his ladder when she walked into the derelict building.

"Hi everyone," said Jeremy gently. "This is my daughter Daisy. She's just come to check up on us, make sure we're doing a good job."

Daisy stood there in her blue denim jeans, white jumper, and white sneakers, wishing the earth would swallow her whole. It had been such a long time since she had been in the company of admiring men and she just didn't know what to do. Where was she supposed to look? What was she supposed to say? She found herself completely tongue-tied.

Her granddad sidled up to her and put his arm around her shoulder.

"It's alright love, we won't let any of these charming chaps whisk you off your feet!"

His comment broke the ice and everyone laughed—even the young men who had been planning to try exactly that.

Suddenly, it seemed that everyone had something they needed to talk to Jeremy about. It amused him to see how much they all wanted to consult with him today, just so they could get close to Daisy. Usually they just got on with their work quietly; this wasn't the kind of building site where loud, popular music blared all day long or workmen shouted obscenities across the room. Usually these men worked quietly, each intent on his own task. These were craftsmen, skilled experts in their fields.

There were expert plasterers, carpenters, and metalworkers, all men who had chosen to learn a skill that was quickly dying out.

The young man who had almost fallen off the ladder staring at Daisy was an incredible plasterer. He was working on the ornate cornices running around the top of the high ceilings. Over the years, the original ones had been badly damaged and in places, there was almost nothing left of the elaborate and intricate carving.

He was painstakingly cutting out the damaged bits and measuring carefully to ensure that the new mouldings he made would be an exact fit.

"Great job, Phil."

Jeremy had come to stand beside his daughter as she gazed up at the lofty ceilings the young man was working on.

"Oh thanks, Jeremy. This room is proving a bit harder than the rest. I think when it was modernised they weren't very careful about how they covered it up. It's a shame, because some of the patterns in here are the best in the house. Much fancier than the others."

"I suppose that means you'll be charging us more, then?"

Both men laughed.

"You know me, Jeremy. Always charge a fair price! Mind you, this lot is a bit tricky. It will take me a while to get the moulds right. It's not a stock standard you see, not in any of the old catalogues, so I'm just going to have to make it up. But I can do it, don't you worry. Those clients of yours will never be able to tell the old bits from the new ones when I'm finished."

Daisy wandered around the old building, admiring all the features and lamenting all the damaged bits. She had seen places like this one many times, places that some people thought were only fit for demolition. Somehow though, her dad and grandad, together with all these skilled craftsmen, managed to restore the buildings to their former glory.

"I think I might go for a stroll along the seafront, Dad. I could use some exercise and fresh air. Maybe I'll even go up to the Old Town and pop into some of the shops."

"Actually, I've got to go up to the Old Town to collect some bits. Shall I give you a lift, Daisy?"

The young man looked at her longingly.

"No thanks, Phil. That's really kind of you, but I think a walk will do me good."

All the men, including her father and grandfather, watched her as she carefully made her way out of the scaffolded building. When she reached the wide open space of the gardens they were still watching her. However, she was completely oblivious to everyone's admiring glances. Henry had destroyed all her self-confidence; she had absolutely no idea of the charm she possessed anymore.

It took a while to reach the Old Town. It was a lovely sunny day, but a bit chilly with a breeze blowing across the English Channel. Daisy enjoyed the walk, she knew the place so well. She wandered past the pier and past the old White Rock Theatre, where she chuckled at the poster proclaiming the next event: *The Fantastic Hastings Summer Variety Show*. This was the same show she insisted on being taken to see every year since she was a little girl. She had always loved the theatre, the bright lights, the fancy costumes, the larger-than-life characters. She had always imagined herself on the stage, performing to an audience of thousands, with loud applause greeting her every performance. But in reality, she was too shy to go on stage and too lacking in self-confidence. Even at school she had been too shy to audition for the annual productions, unsure if she was pretty or talented enough. Her teachers had been cross—they had seen what a natural performer she was—because of course she was beautiful *and* talented, certainly enough for any leading lady role.

She continued wandering along the seafront, enjoying the smell of the ozone from the sea and the gentle breeze blowing across the pebbly beach. She remembered long lazy days spent playing there, collecting big bags full of pebbles and rocks to take back to London. Her bedroom had been full of such treasures, precious things collected on every trip she went. By the time she was eight years old she had so many different collections—shells, pebbles, rocks, feathers, and small bits of driftwood—that her dad had designed her a special storage area: one whole wall of her bedroom was fitted out with wooden shelves of different lengths.

"Why aren't they all the same, Dad?"

"Well, my darling, this is what you call architecture, making things look more interesting, less ordinary. Using a bit of flair to produce something different. Something that people will look at and admire, not just a bit of old flat-pack junk. "

Daisy smiled, remembering the conversation. How her dad detested flat-pack furniture. How he said it had "taken away people's individuality and made them all clones, all identical."

She was still thinking about it as she strolled along, and seeing a pretty girl with a smile on her face made other people smile too. She was greeted by the postman on his bike, two small boys kicking a football on the grassy verge, an old lady pulling along a flowery shopping trolley, and a bunch of workmen loitering outside a new building site. They were all laughing and smoking cigarettes, but as Daisy passed by there was a hush as they all stared at her, mesmerised by her youth and beauty. One of the younger ones wolf-whistled and she blushed a little, unused to such open admiration.

"Hello, darling. Do you fancy coming out for a drink with me tonight?"

His mates all chuckled as Daisy turned 'round, smiled sweetly at him, and said in her quiet, well-spoken London voice "Thank you so much, but I'm afraid I'm busy tonight."

His workmates all chuckled at his crestfallen face.

"Oh come on mate, why would a beautiful, posh young lady want to go out with a ruffian like you?"

Daisy felt sorry for the young man. She knew what rejection felt like, what it felt like to have someone tell you that you weren't good enough.

She turned back and flashed him a shy smile. His mates all poked him and his face reddened. Her kindness made him brave.

"Okay then, maybe see you tomorrow instead."

Somehow that chance encounter made her feel better, better about herself, about the future. Perhaps she was good enough, after all. Perhaps one day, she would fall in love all over again.

By the time she reached the Old Town, Daisy was pretty exhausted. She had forgotten quite how far it was. She wandered over to the Stade, the shingle beach, to see all the fishing boats return with their catch. She stopped, as always, to admire the net houses, the tall, skinny, black wooden buildings that had always fascinated her. She smiled as she passed the funfair, remembering how many happy hours she had spent there as a little girl. She would drag her mum, dad, and grandparents onto every ride. Her favourite had been the Whirling Cups and Saucers ride, where enormous metal objects gaudily painted in shades of cerise pink, violet, lime green, citrus yellow, and cherry red awaited them. Each huge cup and saucer was decorated with large, contrasting coloured flowers, and the overall effect was of a mad psychedelic tea party.

THE SECOND DAISY

She had also loved the Caterpillar rollercoaster. It had a gigantic bright green cartoon caterpillar at the front and each carriage was designed to look like part of his body. She remembered screaming and hanging onto her dad for dear life as the coaster hurtled around each bend. Looking at it now she realised how small it was, how low to the ground, designed for toddlers and small children. She smiled at the little ones climbing aboard and nodded knowingly to the adults accompanying them. Some of those kids looked just as scared as she used to be!

Leaving behind the familiar noise and smells of the funfair, the fried onions from the hotdogs, the sweetness from the candy floss and hot doughnuts, the greasy smell of the frying fish and chips, she crossed the main road.

Hastings Old Town was one of her favourite places. Narrow, winding, cobbled streets and little shops filled the area. Quite different from the modern shopping precinct just up the road, this was a place where hundreds of years of life was exposed. History came to life in the old brickwork, the stone, and the ancient nooks and crannies.

Overlooked by two hills, East Hill and West Hill, the picturesque jumble of streets was full of old antique shops, little grocers, florists, pubs, and cafés where weather-beaten locals gathered to drink and gossip.

When she was younger, Daisy had loved going on the old funicular railway that whisked you up the hillside. On the western side were the castle ruins from the castle that had been built after the Battle of Hastings in 1066. On the top of East Hill Daisy had loved to roam the wide open spaces, including a beautiful park-like area with the most stunning views of the Channel. On a bright, clear day, she'd often been quite sure that she could see across the ocean, right to France.

She sat outside a little café, enjoying the sunshine on her face. The enormous mug of tea she had been served was in a chunky, slightly-chipped brown china mug, but even that slight imperfection didn't detract from her joy. Somehow, being here in this familiar place, a place she had never once visited with Henry, made her calm.

"For God's sake, Daisy, why on earth do you want to go to that dump?

Hastings may have been nice back in its time, but now it's just a miserable, tatty place with nothing to recommend it. Unless you like pie and mash or stale beer and winkles!"

She had always wanted to correct him, to tell him of the town's charm, its endearing features and excellent fresh fish. Somehow though, she knew he wouldn't listen; he wasn't interested in her views. Therefore, they had always gone to Brighton for their outings.

"Much better class of people and of course, we can stay in your family's place."

Despite having little or nothing to do with Daisy's family, he was not averse to using the Brighton townhouse. It was a beautiful Regency building in one of Brighton's finest crescents, right on the seafront. The house was Old Frederick Palmer's; he had bought it in the 1930s and it had now been passed down through the family to Daisy's grandparents.

"People are always terribly impressed when I tell them we have a house on Royal Crescent. Must be worth a million or so now, I reckon. Maybe if Joe and Flo ever decide to sell, we can have first refusal?"

At times like that, she rather hated Henry. How dare he talk about their treasured family home like that, as if it was just another financial transaction that he could make money from? But of course, intimidated by him as she was, she never aired those feelings. Instead, each time she submitted meekly to his wishes, and asked GG Flo if they could borrow the Brighton house yet again.

After finishing her enormous cup of tea she decided she was rather peckish, so she ordered another cup and a huge cheese scone to go with it. The scone turned out to be a bit dry with not nearly enough cheese, but she didn't care. Just being here in the sunshine, listening to the shrill cries of the seagulls, knowing she was free from Henry—free from his constant grumbling—was enough. Enough to make her feel lighter, freer, *almost* able to imagine enjoying life again.

"Are you looking for anything special, my love?"

She turned to smile at the owner of the little shop. It was so crowded inside that it looked like Aladdin's cave—except that Aladdin's cave was full of treasures and this one was mostly full of junk.

"Not really, thanks. I'm just browsing—if that's okay?"

"'Course it is, my girl. On your own today? Where's your old granddad?"

Usually Daisy went foraging in the shops with Sam. He was a wonderful companion and they had been doing it since she was a little girl, rummaging around the old junk and antique shops looking for treasure.

"Oh, he's working with my dad! They're overseeing the renovation of some of those old houses in Warrior Square."

The owner of the shop smiled at the pretty girl in front of him. Daisy was still beautiful of course, but somehow she seemed different from the last time he had seen her. Quieter, with a real sadness about her.

Daisy roamed around the shop, stopping every few minutes to pick up something and examine it carefully. Every so often she peered over a pile of old china or a box full of books and found the old man staring at her. It didn't make her feel uncomfortable at all, she had known him since she was tiny, knew his history, knew his sorrows.

She remembered that he had told her granddad about how in 1937, when he was just six years old, his father had sent him to England with the pretext of improving his language skills. His father had been astute enough to see what was coming and wanted his only son safely out of the way, away from Germany and the horrors of war. However, he had not been quite astute enough to realise that anyone like them—a Jew—would be in such mortal danger. Daisy remembered how the old man, whose name was Eli, had wept when he told them how his entire family, every single one of them left in Germany, had perished in the concentration camps. He grieved them all still, more than 50 years later, and had never allowed himself to love again, constantly fearful of losing them, too.

He watched as Daisy roamed around his shop. He loved the way she was so careful with all his stock. The store's goods were piled high, filling every single nook and cranny. While some people might call his things rubbish, to Eli, the store's contents were his whole life. He had bought the freehold of the little shop in 1957 and intended to stay there until he died.

"Mr. Eli?" Daisy had been brought up to treat her elders with respect and rarely used their first names.

"Yes, my love?"

Do you think my Nana Winifred would like this bowl? She was holding up a beautiful red glass bowl. It had obviously seen better days, as it had a slight crack on one side.

"Oh Miss Daisy, you do have good taste. Your Nana would love it, I think. A nice piece of good Murano glass. It would have cost a pretty penny when it was new, but now, with that crack, I could only charge you a couple of quid."

Daisy laughed. She had always enjoyed bartering with the old man.

He had explained the system of bartering to her one day years ago, when she and her granddad were looking through his stock.

"Now little miss, the idea is that I start by naming an exorbitant price..."

"What does exorbitant mean, Mr. Eli?"

Her granddad had snorted in the background.

"What he means, Daisy, is that the first price he says is about twice as much as he really expects people to pay. He's just an old crook really, so don't fall for his charming sales patter!"

She had recently seen the film *Oliver,* and that was the first time she had realised that Eli was Jewish. In fact, he did look rather like Fagin, but she knew he was a good man unlike the fictional character.

In the years since, Daisy had become rather good at bartering. Eli and her granddad had taught her well.

"Well, I do think Nana would like it; it would look really nice on her sideboard. But, it's definitely not worth two pounds. What about 75 pence?"

"Come on, Miss Daisy, how do you expect an old man to make enough money to feed himself? If I gave in to such outrageous offers, I'd be dead of starvation in a week! That fine old piece of glass is definitely worth at least one pound fifty."

"Nonsense, Mr. Eli. No one else will want to buy it with this big crack in it. My Nana will love it because I chose it, but she'll still have to turn it 'round to hide the crack. How about one pound?"

"One pound twenty five is my lowest offer and that is *killing* me. How do you expect me to pay my rent this week?"

Daisy laughed. Everyone knew that he had owned the old property for years and he certainly didn't pay rent for anything. He slept in the room at the back of the shop and never bothered to cook anything in the shabby little kitchen—he just popped to the local café for all his meals, leaving a handwritten sign on the door saying *"BACK IN HALF AN HOUR OR SO."*

"Okay, deal. One pound twenty five it is. But I need to keep on looking in case I find some other overpriced treasure!"

In the end, Daisy left the little shop over an hour later, laden down with her purchases. Along with the glass bowl, she had bought a couple of old books for her granddad and a basket full of old wooden cotton reels, some still with the original thread attached. She was certain that GG Flo would be thrilled with them; in fact, she probably already had a pile of them in those old shop cupboards of hers.

The old man had been a little bemused when she had picked them out, but once she explained who they were for, he understood. Flo was a great favourite of his. He always enjoyed her visits. She was always as enthusiastic about his mountains of old stock as her great-granddaughter was today.

"And how is the lovely Florence? Please send her my best regards and tell her I miss seeing her beautiful face."

Daisy smiled to herself. She had always known that the old Jewish man had a soft spot for GG.

"Now that I know those old cotton reels are desirable to someone as special as Florence, I might have to consider putting the price up. But I'll tuck the rest of them away up here in my secret little cupboard, just in case she fancies some more. Just tell her to give me a call."

As she hugged the old man goodbye, Daisy realised how thin he was, much thinner than the last time she had seen him. They all worried about him a bit. He had no-one, no family at all, no-one to take care of him in his old age. Occasionally he shut the shop for a few days and came up to London to stay in Artillery Passage, but despite the kindness shown to him and his pleasure in spending time in Flo's company, he never settled for long. He insisted he never wanted to be a nuisance, to outstay his welcome. Once he had come for Christmas and it had been such a happy joyful time, but somehow, being amongst such a loving family had made him feel lonelier. He never accepted the offer again. Instead, he looked forward to the family's infrequent visits to Hastings, thoroughly enjoying their company but with no need to make any sort of commitment. His own family members were long dead and gone, and sometimes he felt as though the biggest part of him had died in the camps, too.

After leaving Eli's cramped and crowded little shop, Daisy wandered through the lanes, stopping to admire items in the shop windows as she passed. Perhaps tomorrow she would come back with her dad and look at that old rosewood writing bureau. She had always fancied one, but she had no idea whether the one in the shop window was good—whether it was a genuine antique or just a good fake reproduction. Not to mention, it was pretty pricey at 200 pounds. The piece was way out of her price range really, but she knew that her dad and granddad would buy it for her if she really wanted it.

The last building she popped into was the old second-hand bookshop. She had been going in there since she was a little girl and knew the owner well.

"Hello, Mrs. Jones. How are you today?"

THE SECOND DAISY

Emily Jones looked up from the table where she had been pricing a pile of old books.

"Daisy, my darling girl. How are you? Have you brought your lovely granddad with you?"

Emily Jones was a spinster of indeterminate age. She had probably once been a real beauty, but like a lot of naturally blonde, beautiful women, the years had not been particularly kind to her. She was probably now in her early 60s and in exchange for her fading beauty, she had become a little eccentric. Today she was wearing a long red woollen dress, almost down to her ankles. Over this was a green satin waistcoat, embroidered with large flowers in shades of blue and yellow. On her feet she wore orange gumboots. Her once blonde hair was dyed bright red, almost as red as her dress, and she wore large tortoiseshell glasses which had slipped to the end of her rather small nose.

She caught Daisy staring at her feet.

"Oh I know these boots don't go with my outfit, but I just popped over to the fish market and got some nice prawns for my tea. Got a bit of haddock for tomorrow's breakfast, too."

Like Eli, Emily lived over her shop, so her whole life revolved around the Old Town. Her father had established the bookshop when he was a young man, more than 70 years earlier in the 1920s, and she had inherited it when he died. She had never intended to end her life as a lonely old spinster running a dilapidated old bookshop, but the man she had loved since she was a schoolgirl—an accountant from Bexhill—had broken her heart by running off with her best friend. By the time she got over that heartbreak, her father was dying and she had moved to Hastings to care for him. And somehow, she had never left.

She lived upstairs in a rather shambolic flat. Daisy had been up there a few times and was shocked by the mountains of books and papers on every surface. And the cats. There had been at least four of them, big, fat, ginger cats sitting atop the piles.

"How are your cats, Mrs. Jones?"

"Oh, you know Daisy, there's always a few around. They all seem to have kittens every five minutes, I just can't keep up with them all."

Despite the cats and the fact that the bookshop was packed solid with books of every kind, the atmosphere was quite tranquil. Perfumed candles and joss sticks created a pleasant smell that wafted around the room, eliminating any slight cat or otherwise musty odours. Daisy had always worried about the fire risk of these, but Emily had assured her there was absolutely no danger of them setting fire to the place.

"If I had wanted to burn this place down I would have done it years ago. Now it's too late; this old shop is part of me. If it burned down now I reckon I would die too."

"Anyway my love, it's lovely to see you. I expect you've been over the road, chatting up that old devil Eli, haven't you?"

It was a well-known fact among the residents of the Old Town that Emily had carried a torch for Eli for many years. Sadly though, he had never noticed, and she was far too shy to ever say anything to him. So, they had just remained friends—good friends who often went to the pub together or ate cheese on toast in Emily's kitchen, but they had never exchanged a romantic, loving word... and certainly not a kiss. Sometimes, in her lonely bed, Emily would fantasise about how wonderful their life together could have been, could still be, if only she was a little more confident and he wasn't so closed up, so unwilling to let his feelings out.

"Yes, I have been over at Mr. Eli's and I got some real bargains. Do you want to see?

There was no-one else in the shop, so Emily cleared a space on the table and Daisy laid out her purchases.

"I suppose he fleeced you for all this? How much did the old devil charge you?"

Emily spoke with affection in her voice. She knew exactly how much Eli loved little Daisy, how much they all loved her and how angry they had all been to hear how badly Henry had treated her.

By the time Daisy had shown off all her purchases, drunk a cup of sweet milky tea from an old chipped china cup (a rather beautiful Clarice Cliff Art Deco design that had seen better days), eaten a huge slice of coffee and walnut cake, and got caught up on all the Old Town gossip, it was almost time to leave.

"Dad said he would pick me up and drive me back to the hotel when they've finished at the site. I guess he knew I'd end up with a few parcels to carry."

At that moment, the shop doorbell rang.

Emily had it installed a couple of years earlier in an attempt to repel any unwanted shoplifters. In her father's day he had rarely suffered any such losses, but over the years she had often found gaps on the bookshelves where people had sneaked into the shop while she was busy upstairs. At first, she hadn't worried too much. If people were that desperate to read, then she was happy to supply them with the odd book or two. But one day, she realised that ten of her best, most expensive antiquarian books were gone. These were old, valuable books worth over a hundred pounds each, books her father had acquired over the years that she was just hanging onto, waiting for the right person to buy and cherish them.

Eli had been the one to insist she got the bell.

"Look Emily, those thugs could come back anytime, and one day they might decide to bash you over the head as well as steal all your good stuff. I really think you should do it. You could get one of those bells under the doormat, the kind that makes noise every time someone walks in."

Jeremy and Samuel seemed to bring the cold in with them. The sun had gone down by now and the ocean breeze seemed much chillier than it had a couple of hours earlier.

"Hello you gorgeous creature, how are you doing?"

Samuel enveloped Emily in a warm hug and the older woman beamed. It was very rare nowadays that she got so much as a glance from any man, let alone a handsome chap like this.

She wriggled reluctantly from his arms.

"Oh Sam, whatever would your Win say if she could see you now?"

"She would say that I am a very lucky man to have such a beautiful woman in my arms, and that I better treat you right—or else!"

They all laughed. Everyone knew that Samuel adored his wife and would never stray, but they also knew what an old charmer he was and how he loved to flirt.

"So Daisy, should we have brought the pick-up truck to carry all your purchases?"

Daisy smiled lovingly at her dad.

"I think so, Dad. I just couldn't resist any of it. And I've found a couple of really good books here, too. Emily always has such wonderful stuff. And I got some bits for Nana's collection too, from Mr. Eli."

"Well while you're making us a nice cup of tea Emily, why don't Jeremy and I have a browse through your stock, just in case there's anything we fancy too?"

By the time their short visit was over, Jeremy had bought three enormous architecture books and Sam had found a 1930s book about America and the Great Depression. They bade a fond farewell to Emily, promising to return with the rest of the family very soon. Then, the three of them returned to the Royal Victoria—laden down with all their purchases.

THE BIG ADVENTURE

In an effort to cheer Daisy up following her traumatic divorce, Melissa proposed a trip for all of them, to America.

She wanted them to sail there on the QE2, the luxury liner owned by Cunard.

Her treat.

Although Melissa was now in her 90th year, you would think she was only 70. She had kept her slim figure, her hair was dyed a discreet strawberry blonde, and she was always impeccably dressed and made up. It helped, of course, that she had never had to worry about money; she owned the mansion flat in Bloomsbury *and* had a large trust fund.

"Now, before you all make a fuss, please let me speak."

Despite living in England for almost 70 years, Melissa still spoke with a distinctive Alabama accent.

"I want to go back and see my homeland one more time before I die, and I am far too old to make the trip alone. Having all of you there will make it much more bearable, and I daresay we will have a bit of fun."

Despite her advancing years, she was still very good at having fun.

She, Matty, and Ruth had always hosted wonderful parties, and still did, although they were a little more restrained these days. Now it was just cocktails, jazz, and conversation.

In the end, after much discussion, nearly all of them agreed to go on the trip.

John and Nigel from Nottingham decided to take early retirement and join them, although they insisted on paying for their part of the trip themselves.

Jeremy and Samuel agreed to close the office for six weeks and Vi booked all the annual leave she had accrued for the last three years.

Flo and Polly decided that the dress shop could be closed while they were away; after all, their clientele was very loyal. Anyway, they were sure to pick up some inspiration for new designs during their travels.

Daisy was beyond herself with excitement, particularly when Nana Winifred reminded her that when the ship docked in New York, they would go straight to Harlem to catch up with all the relatives there.

The only ones who weren't keen on leaving were Joe, Matty, and Ruth. They all felt that they were a bit too old to go gallivanting around the world.

Melissa was tearful when they told her.

"But, I wanted you all there. It just won't be the same without you."

In the end, it was agreed that Ruth would go. After all, she had been looking after Melissa since she was a baby, why should she stop now? And it would be lovely to go back to the plantation to see her family.

But Matty was adamant.
"I did all my travelling when I was a young man. When Theo and I did our Grand Tour. You know how it upset me when we went back to Alabama in 1927, and I was just a young man then. I don't want to do it anymore. Joe and I will do very well. I will move into Artillery Passage while you're all away and we will have a fine old time, won't we Joe? No nagging wives, put our feet up on the sofas, watch the football. It will be marvellous."

Joe puffed on his pipe and smiled. Matty was a lot braver than him, he would never have had the nerve to stand up to Melissa like that. But he was right. They were both old men now and would do very well home alone—just as long as someone brought them some decent meals. They wouldn't last very long just eating his ginger cake!

And so it was decided.

Plans were made, crossings were booked, and there was a flurry of dressmaking. After all, seven women couldn't be expected to embark on a transatlantic crossing without a whole new wardrobe each!

There had never been such a flurry of activity in Flo's little dress shop. Everywhere you looked, there were rolls of beautiful fabrics—in all the colours of the rainbow and made of every possible fibre you could imagine—stacked up against every available bit of wall space.

There were rolls of fine Scottish tweed, linen from Ireland in every conceivable shade, poplin, cotton, velvet, silk, satin, lace, and corduroy.

Seven women, all with different ideas of what their ideal holiday wardrobe should look like.

Flo smiled as she looked around the room at the women she loved most in the world. She was just sad that both her mum, the original Daisy, and her Aunty Sybil weren't still alive to join in the fun. Most especially, she was sad that neither of them had ever got to meet their little Daisy. How they would have loved her.

She glanced across to where Daisy was sitting on the old wooden floor. Planning this trip had certainly perked her up a bit, but she still looked very pale and wan. The last few years had really taken away her sparkle.

Hopefully this wonderfully generous gesture of Melissa's to take them all away on such a fabulous trip would bring back their lovely girl: the bright, shiny, enthusiastic person she had been before her doomed marriage.

None of them would ever really know the whole truth of what had gone on; Daisy was far too proud to tell them. Not to mention that Nigel, her solicitor and Great-Uncle John's partner, had promised that he would never, ever, betray her confidence.

She had told him so much, things that rather horrified him, about the way Henry had treated her. She told him of the neglect, the emotional bullying, and his disloyalty. How he had cheated on her so many times.

As a divorce lawyer, Nigel always kept a box of tissues handy on his desk. Daisy, who almost never cried in public, went through almost a whole box of these as she told him her sorry tale.

"Oh John, listening to Daisy today, and all the other women I see with similar stories about their brutes for husbands just makes me so glad I have you."

The two men were sitting in the beautiful, very tastefully decorated lounge of their old farmhouse, just outside

Nottingham. They had bought the house when they first got together, nearly twenty years earlier.

Nigel and John had met through mutual friends. They had both been single, rather shy men who had never allowed themselves to experience true love with another man until the day when their eyes met over the dinner table. On that day they talked for hours, realising they had, at last, found a kindred spirit in one another. They had been so happy ever since sharing their lives, although they were always so discreet that many people assumed they were friends, rather than lovers.

"Well, I'm just glad our Daisy has got you to fight in her corner. I know you will get her free from that horrible man as soon as you possibly can."

Sometimes it seemed to John that his real life hadn't started until he met Nigel.

He had realised that he preferred men rather than pretty young girls when he first left London and went to university. There had been a few unsuitable dalliances and he had been left heartbroken many times, so much so that he had vowed to remain celibate all his life. Like Old Frederick Palmer and young Fred had.

As a young man, he had sometimes, on his infrequent trips back to London and after seeing the family in Artillery Passage, gone to spend a few days with the two old men. Those two old men, part of his family, who had been together as soulmates in a very loving but celibate relationship for almost fifty years. How he used to envy them.

And now he had Nigel, the love of his life.

The two men sipped their whisky, both deep in thought.

"Well, I guess if these women are getting themselves dolled up with new wardrobes, perhaps we had better do the same. Shall we pop up to town for a little shopping spree this weekend?"

"I'm so glad that we have decided to go with them. I can't wait to see New York and Harlem. Samuel has promised to take us to some jazz clubs."

"And Melissa and Ruth can't wait to show us Alabama, although I daresay we will have to mind our Ps and Qs if her nephew starts talking about any tricky subjects."

Both men, who had suffered personally because of their sexual leanings, abhorred any form of injustice, particularly racism. Thus, they were slightly anxious about how their visit to the Deep South would be, to visit Melissa and Ruth's old home. Melissa from the grand plantation house and Ruth from the old slave quarters in the garden. It certainly promised to be an interesting trip.

THE JOURNEY

There had been tearful goodbyes at Artillery Passage. The minibus driver had been very patient as everyone hugged and kissed the two old men standing in the shop doorway.

"Whew, I thought they would never leave."
"I know. It looked like Ruth and Flo were going to change their minds about going at all."

It was true. Once all the preparations and excitement of planning and packing were done, Ruth and Flo began to doubt the wisdom of leaving their husbands behind.

"Oh Ruth, I've hardly ever had a day away from Joe since we got married. After 68 years together, I'm not sure if he'll manage on his own."

"I know, Flo. I feel the same about leaving Matty. He's been my rock all these years, it will feel strange without him. At the same time, I remember how unhappy our last trip to Alabama made him. It brought back so many bad memories and I don't want to see him hurt again, but I'm really worried about something happening to him, or your Joe, while we're away."

Finally, the minibus, laden down with the weight of all of them and their copious amounts of luggage, turned the corner and was gone from sight. Both men wiped away the tears that were pouring down their old, wrinkled faces and turned to go inside, making sure to put the CLOSED sign on the glass shop door.

They looked at each other and smiled sadly, two old men, one Black and one White, who had been close friends now for almost 70 years.

"At least we've got that lovely Emma and her mum keeping an eye on us."

Both men chuckled. Although the years had taken a toll on their bodies, in their heads, Joe was still the virile young docker and Matty the very attractive nightclub saxophone player. Not to mention that young Emma and her mum, who owned the little café next door, were both very pretty women!

Artillery Passage had become very gentrified lately.
When Flo and Joe had first moved there as a young married couple back in the 1920s, it had been in a working class area. It was one step above the surrounding slums but a bit rough nevertheless, with the docks close by.

Nowadays, it, like much of the East End of London, had seen a lot of changes.

The beautiful old five-storey brick houses fronting right onto the cobbled street seemed unchanged from the outside, but inside was a different story. They had originally been built in the 1700s for Huguenot silk merchants. Over the years they had seen many changes of fortune, and now most of them had been ripped apart and converted into apartments. However, they almost all had the original shopfronts—the lovely old glass flattened bow windows, so characteristic of the period.

At one time, when Flo and Joe had first moved in, the street had been crowded, bustling even. As well as Flo's dress shop, there had been an old public house on the corner, a little grocer's shop, and even a cigar manufacturer. Now, the area had become quite gentrified. The pub was still there on the corner but the spit and sawdust had gone, replaced by a trendy bistro menu, and the place was constantly packed with office workers and tourists, rather than locals. The little grocer's shop was long gone, unable to keep up with the convenience and low prices offered by the big supermarket chains. The cigar shop had closed down in 1935 and that building had remained empty for many years, sinking into disrepair, but was recently bought by a developer and was now all scaffolded up. It was patiently waiting to be turned into a desirable residence for some rich young Londoner.

The old grocer's shop was now a modern little café called The Banana Box, owned by Emma and her mum. The inside walls were painted in varying shades of bright yellow. Large wooden crates had been turned into tables, and on every wall there were photos of the old docks, which were closed down many years ago and no longer in use (some of them were being turned into office blocks and fancy dockside apartments). The Banana Box Café was a warm, inviting, and cosy place, and Joe had spent many happy hours there, chatting to the two ladies, eating their delicious food, and regaling any interested customers with stories of his days working at St. Katharine's Docks. Therefore, it had seemed very sensible to ask the two ladies to keep an eye on Joe and Matty while the rest of the family was away.

John and Nigel had driven down from Nottingham and were waiting for the women at the docks in Southampton, and as she descended from the minibus and looked around at her extended family, Daisy felt herself relaxing.

Six whole weeks, having adventures with her beloved family. Seeing New York and meeting her dad's relatives from Harlem for the first time. What a wonderful time they would all have together. All the bad memories of her short, miserable marriage seemed to recede as she stared in awe at the magnificent ship.

The QE2 was certainly a splendid ship.

They all had staterooms on the upper deck. Melissa had been determined that this, her final trip to the land of her birth, would be memorable for them all, so she had booked the best possible suites with absolutely no expense spared.

Melissa, Ruth, Flo, and Vi were sharing one of the largest penthouse suites, with a huge balcony that gave them magnificent views of the ocean. There were three bedrooms, each with their own bathroom and a large sitting room.

Melissa and Ruth shared one room by choice.

Ruth, who had looked after Melissa since she was a baby, could not bear to see the younger woman struggling to do up the zips on her dresses with her arthritic fingers, or trying desperately to open a new jar of face cream with a difficult lid. To save Melissa's feelings, she had pretended that she wanted them to share a room because she would miss Matty. But they all knew the truth. She had loved and cared for Melissa all her life—since they were young girls on the cotton plantation—and even though they were both in their dotage, nothing was going to stop Ruth from taking care of her now.

John and Nigel obviously had their own large suite, as did Samuel and Winifred. They were all quite overcome with the splendour of it all.

Daisy was delighted to see that the enormous two-bedroomed suite she was sharing with her mum and dad was almost as huge as Melissa's, with the same stunning ocean views.

As they walked into the Queen's Grill and Lounge on their first night onboard, both Melissa and Ruth remembered the first time they had crossed the Atlantic back in 1922.

It was just a year after Melissa had been widowed, suddenly and without warning. Their beloved Theo, her husband and the much-loved best friend of Matty, had dropped dead, breaking their hearts. They had travelled to England a year later on a whim planning for just a short holiday, but they had never returned to Alabama. Instead, they chose to make London their permanent home.

That first trip, so long ago now, had been on another Cunard liner. The journey, on the Berengaria, was etched in Melissa's and Ruth's mind. It had been a pleasant, but rather upsetting crossing. It came with the shock of realising that racial prejudice was not confined to the States, but was also rife among wealthy Europeans.

It came with the indignity of being asked by a fellow passenger to leave Ruth and Matty in their quarters at mealtimes so as not to upset the other guests, just because of their black skins.

Melissa had been absolutely furious then, and Ruth still remembered how desperately uncomfortable she had been entering the dining room every night after that, enduring the stares and disapproval of their fellow passengers.

This trip was different, thank God.

For a start, Melissa had spent an absolute fortune on all their passages, so that alone made her something of a celebrity in the eyes of the crew.

And there were eleven of them, almost an entire army, should anyone care to take them on.

Their group consisted of two tall handsome Black men, two, not quite so tall, but very distinguished White men, and seven magnificent women: Melissa, Flo, Vi, and Polly (all

White and very forceful), Ruth and Winifred (two beautiful, mature Black women), and Daisy, the youngest of them all. Daisy, a beautiful coffee-coloured girl with magnificent dark brown curls and hazel eyes.

The first night, at the captain's table was a very happy one.

Daisy's family group obviously occupied most of the gilt chairs, but in addition, handpicked by the captain himself, there was a charming couple from Baltimore: an extremely good-looking and charming Black doctor and his Harvard-educated, beautiful White wife. They seemed delighted to share their first evening with such an interesting family group, as did the rather shy retired marine biologist, the art dealer and his glamorous wife from Chicago, and the retired Spanish architect and his beautiful, much younger Italian wife from Barcelona.

The conversation (and the wine) flowed freely all evening, and the other guests in the dining room looked longingly over at the main table, wishing that they too had been considered important enough to join such an illustrious group.

Daisy, who was by far the youngest, looked around at everyone seated at the table, all only stopping to either eat some of the delicious food or take a sip or two of the champagne, wine, or cocktails placed in front of them. She was happy to just listen, mostly. She didn't really feel she had much to contribute, and she certainly didn't want to talk about her lack of career or failed marriage.

"Isn't this just marvellous, Daisy darling?" Melissa spoke in her soft Southern drawl.

"Who would have believed we would end up with such a fine, wonderful family?"

Melissa still marvelled at how her family had turned out.

She had grown up as a rather spoilt, cosseted little girl, living on her father's cotton plantation in Alabama. There had been fine clothes, ponies, and every possible whim satisfied by the large group of Black servants the family employed. Some of these servants were descended from the original family slaves, and in Melissa's opinion even as a young girl, they were treated little better than the slaves who had to work outdoors.

It had been such a joy to meet and marry her Theo. He was a man who had also been born into plantation life, a life of excess, but who, like her, strongly rejected the notion that the colour of your skin should make a difference in how you were treated.

She had loved him so dearly, so passionately, despite their age difference—he was 35 to her 19 when they married—and she had been utterly bereft when he suddenly died of a heart attack just one year after their wedding. They had not even had time to have a baby and start a family of their own. Without the love and support of Ruth and Matty, Melissa knew she would have just given up, retreated into her shell, stayed in the big mansion on the plantation as a sad, bitter, and lonely widow.

She looked around the table and her eyes rested on Ruth. Her beloved Ruth. It was Ruth who had been looking after Melissa all her life, and now, decades later, she still was. Ruth was her rock, her joy, and her comfort. Matty had looked after them both all these years, and although she was disappointed he wasn't with them on this trip, she understood.

She would never forget the pain in his eyes the last time they visited, when they had gone back to Alabama for her grandfather's funeral in 1927.

It had been a strange visit. Although prohibition was still in place in America at that time, her father still managed to have a full liquor cabinet and of course, the alcohol loosened peoples tongues.

"Why the hell are you wearing those improper clothes?"
"Short skirts, no corsets."
"And smoking!"
"Isn't it time you got a decent man to take care of you?"
"Settle down like a good Southern girl, not all this wild living like you seem to be doing."
"And in the wrong company."

Melissa knew that "the wrong company" they were referring to was Ruth and Matty.

Her family had never understood and certainly never approved of the closeness she felt to them. Luckily, neither of them had been there to hear such nasty talk, they had both been staying with their families in the old slave quarters in the garden. Her family would certainly not have allowed them to stay in the main house, despite the fact that they shared the mansion flat in London with her.

She was so glad they hadn't been privy to all that hateful racist and bigoted talk. At the same time, she just hated to see the sadness in Ruth and Matty's eyes. Sadness because they realised that, although their new lives in London were marvellous and happy, their families back here were still living a life of servitude and poverty with little or no chance of escape. Slavery may have been abolished decades before, but for many Black people, particularly in the South, nothing much had changed. They were still obliged to be at their employers' beck and call.

During the visit so long ago, Matty had been particularly heartbroken over his grandfather, Old Freddie, who had died during his long absence.

Old Freddie had been one of the original slaves on the property and still bore many of the scars from those years.

It turned out that he had kept and treasured every single one of the hundreds of letters that Matty had sent him weekly from London, and that he had read and reread them constantly over the years. Matty wept when he heard this, wept for the loss of his grandfather, and wept too for the lives all the old slaves had been forced to lead, just because of the "accident" of birth.

He remembered Melissa and Theo's words, words he had heard so very many times over the years.

"Just because you are born into a life of poverty, or your skin is black, doesn't make you a lesser person. Some of the best and smartest people I have ever met never got the chance to be their true selves or fulfill all their capabilities and ambitions, just because of the life they were born into."

Melissa understood completely why Matty had decided not to come on this trip. He was an old man now and had no desire whatsoever to be exposed again to such bitter hatred and racism. Much better that he and Joe stayed safely together in Artillery Passage, doing whatever old men choose to do when they are alone and free of womanly supervision.

She turned to look at her oldest and dearest friend. Ruth was still a glorious-looking woman, even in her nineties. She still managed to turn heads wherever she went, and tonight had been no exception. Ruth was looking so elegant, wearing a beautiful full-length pale-yellow silk dress that seemed to ripple around her slim body as she walked. It suited her dark skin so well, and Melissa smiled as she realised that it was almost identical to the one Ruth had worn on that first voyage more than seventy years before.

They had all thoroughly enjoyed planning their wardrobes for this trip and Melissa smiled to herself as she remembered some of the conversations.

"Oh Ruth, do you really think I can get away with this? Don't you think I'm a bit too old to be wearing sparkly stuff?"

It had taken them a while to convince Flo that she certainly wasn't too old to wear anything she fancied. She had spent so many years making beautiful dresses for other women that she had never really bothered to do anything much for herself. Usually, she just wore a simple black or dark-grey dress in the shop, so as not to detract from the gowns the smart society ladies were trying on. When she was at home with Joe, she often just wore her comfy blue tracksuit and some furry slippers!

Looking at her now across the beautifully-laid dining table, her skin glowing in the soft candlelight, Melissa thought that Flo could easily pass for a woman much younger than her 80-something years. She was also wearing a full-length dress, this one made of sparkly lurex material in a soft gold colour. The cowl neckline and three-quarter length sleeves suited her very well. She had designed it herself, of course. Flo had never lost her ability to design the most stunning dresses that any woman would be proud to wear.

Jeremy and Samuel were deep in conversation with the Spanish architect; obviously they had much in common.

"And what do you think about the work of Gaudí? Have you been to Barcelona and seen his work for yourself? If not, I insist you must come. I can show you everything myself. My favourite is the Palau and Parc Güell, the Doric-inspired columns and the colourful mosaic ceiling. And of course, the wonderful dragon fountain. Although there are many other notable buildings, Casa Batiló, for example, with its famous skull and bones balconies. The man was a genius, way ahead of his time."

THE SECOND DAISY

Apart from their common interest in buildings, all three of them were incredibly attractive men and Melissa noticed how the Spanish architect's young wife kept leaning over and touching Jeremy gently on the arm, hoping to gain his attention.

She also noticed how every time this happened, Jeremy looked across the table at Polly, and how, in turn, Polly smiled back at him. A conspiratorial little smile, full of understanding. She knew that women found him attractive and she also knew that he would never stray, that his heart was firmly hers.

Polly looked stunning, as usual. Somehow she never seemed to make much effort, but always managed to look fabulous. Her long black dress was simple and elegant, and she was wearing a beautiful diamond choker around her slim neck. Her blonde curls were piled up on her head and a few tendrils had slipped loose, framing her pretty face.

Melissa had lent her the diamond choker for the trip and intended to insist that she keep it. She would inherit it eventually anyway, so why not have it now while Melissa was still alive to enjoy seeing her wear it? It had been a gift from her daddy in Alabama; he had given it to her on her last trip back in 1927 and it was probably worth a bit. She knew that made no difference to Polly, though. She would have loved it if it came from Woolworths and was worth nothing. Polly had always adored Melissa, even as a very small girl, and therefore she cherished everything that came from the older woman.

Melissa's eyes moved slowly around the table and came to rest on Vi, John, and Nigel, deep in conversation with the art dealer and his wife from Chicago.

It was sad that Vi had never managed to find anyone to love after Bert had deserted her and the girls all those years ago. She was still an attractive woman and could easily find a new partner, but she seemed happy enough, still working and living with her parents in Artillery Passage. She had never moved out, not even during her short, disastrous marriage. Maybe she would meet someone on this trip, there did seem to be a few eligible looking single men on board!

Daisy had changed places with Sam and was now sitting at the far end of the table, next to her Nana Winifred. They made a striking pair.

Winifred had never lost the fine, hourglass figure that had attracted Sam all those years ago, although she did wear a few sizes bigger these days. Tonight she was wearing the most glorious, full-length cerise pink fitted gown that showed every single curve to perfection. She wore no jewellery at all, just a slim gold watch and her wedding band. She looked absolutely magnificent and many of the men in the room could barely keep their eyes off her.

And Daisy. Their little girl. They all loved her deeply and were hoping that this trip would revive her, maybe squash some of the memories of her failed marriage that haunted her. It would be worth every single penny this entire trip had cost if they could only manage to bring back her sparkle—the real Daisy.

Daisy was trying so hard. She knew how very lucky she was to not only have such a supportive family, but to have one that would organise such a fabulous trip just to cheer her up. That was really something.

Tonight she had decided to wear one of the new dresses that GG Flo had designed for her. It was made of beautiful green silk that they had brought back from their trip to India and cut into a simple long sheath dress. The green of the fabric matched her eyes and her dark curly hair was loose, framing her face.

Melissa noticed several young men staring at Daisy, obviously quite overcome by her beauty, but the young woman was oblivious to their glances.
"That damn Henry has taken away all her confidence," Melissa thought crossly to herself.
"We must somehow try to restore it, to make her realise just how lovely and valuable a person she is."

They sat at the captain's table every night of the crossing. Normally he would have passed his favours around, issuing invitations to most of the other first-class passengers, but somehow he could not bear to let the group go, so instead he just got the crew to add more tables. This made the usually sought-after places a welcome addition. The conversations at this table were always lively and varied, and the champagne and fine wine flowed every evening, enhancing people's tongues.

"My, that girl of yours is so damn fine."

"Won't take long for her to get snapped up, I know a couple of Texan millionaires that would kill to have her on their arm."

Daisy did her very best to engage in conversation with her fellow guests, but was totally oblivious to all the compliments flying in her direction. She was much younger than most of the other travellers, and seemed to have little in common with them. She could not talk about her career, her experiences, her children, or even her hopes and dreams. Those hopes and dreams had all been dashed by Henry, the man she had willingly married without really knowing him at all. It hurt her terribly to picture him with Heidi, his new wife, and it hurt even more to imagine them as parents. She had heard about the birth of their son and of their grand wedding. Most of all, she felt a little ashamed that she had been such a bad judge of character and had not listened to the advice of her family. They had all known the marriage was wrong, a disaster in the making, but she had been so determined, so adamant that it was the right thing to do. And now, because of her stubbornness and naivety, here she was, a divorcee before her 22nd birthday with no career or assets to her name. She had no idea that her beauty and kindness were assets beyond measure.

And so the transatlantic crossing continued. Each member of the family was often lost in their own private thoughts, remembering other times, other people, and other lives.

"Well, Vi was right when she said at dinner the other night that this family is certainly the exception to the rule that blood is thicker than water."

They all looked at Jeremy as he spoke. They were nearing the end of the voyage, the ship would be docking in New York the next morning.

They were making the most of their last afternoon at sea, lounging in wooden steamer chairs and looking out at the ocean.

Jeremy shifted in his chair, ensuring they could all hear him properly.

"I was just thinking how lucky we are to have each other. I'm not sure that some of the other passengers can quite work us out. They can't work out who belongs to who and how we all fit together."

Daisy sat upright in her chair. Equality had always been a big topic of conversation in their family, and she loved hearing her dad talk, particularly when it was something he was so passionate about.

NEW YORK, NEW YORK

Melissa had booked a wonderful place for them all to stay in in New York.

"I know you will want to spend time in Harlem, Sam and Win, and of course we are all looking forward to meeting your relatives, but I think it will be much more comfortable if we all stay here together. It is much nicer than booking lots of rooms in some faceless hotel. This way, everyone can do their own thing, spend their days however they'd like, but we can all get together here in between, for breakfasts or dinners. Although I'm not expecting anyone to cook! There are plenty of great restaurants around here we need to try. This is a nice building, very central and big enough for us all to spread out a bit. You could even invite some of the Harlem folk to come and stay here with us for a few days if you like—especially if we are all partying!"

Melissa had every intention of partying. She might be getting on a bit now in years, but in her head she was still a bright young thing, plenty able to cope with a few late nights. She just wished she had visited Studio 54 in New York back in its heyday of the 70s. Some of her Bloomsbury friends had frequented the legendary nightclub on 54th Street and had told her such stories, like the time Bianca Jagger and Liza Minnelli had posed in the nightclub with white doves, or when they mixed with Diana Ross and a young Michael Jackson, or the time they rubbed shoulders with Andy Warhol and Paloma Picasso.

Melissa wished she had been brave enough to do such things herself, to have lived a bit more recklessly.

However, it certainly wasn't too late. She was determined that this, her final big trip, would be wonderful, creating many great memories for all of them.

The place she had chosen for their stay was indeed wonderful. Situated in the heart of Manhattan on the Upper West Side, the Beresford was one of the most prestigious addresses in New York.

It was a splendid 23-storey building dating back to the 1930s, situated between West 81st and 82nd streets.

Melissa had rented three separate apartments in the building, each with three bedrooms and three bathrooms. They were all very luxurious, finished to the highest standard, and she had been lucky enough to hear about them from a friend whose cousin worked in an exclusive real estate office in the city. After having spent a small fortune refurbishing them, the current owner of the apartments was trying to sell them, and was delighted when Melissa offered to rent them all for a couple of weeks at an extortionate amount!

In a way, the Beresford reminded Melissa of her own home in London,

Bedford Court Mansions in Bloomsbury. That was the place she, Ruth, and Matty had established a home when they first moved to London back in the early 20s. It was a place she loved dearly, and was currently rather homesick for.

Of course, the Beresford was much larger and somewhat grander, but there were many similarities: the fine architecture, the spacious, well-appointed rooms, and the charming doormen. It would certainly do very well as their temporary New York base.

On the first afternoon in the city she hired an enormous car, a stretch limo big enough to hold everyone, and they were driven around the city to see all the sights. Most of them had never seen the attractions before, but had only read about them. They included Grand Central Station, the Brooklyn Bridge, Fifth Avenue, Times Square and the Broadway Theatres, Wall Street, Park Avenue, and Madison Square Garden.

Sam and Jeremy were so excited to see all the iconic buildings and admire the stunning architecture—the unusual Flatiron Building, the Chrysler Building, the Empire State building, the Museum of Modern Art, and the Rockefeller Center. They all admired the Woolworth Building, which was built back in 1913, its limestone façade decorated with terracotta.

As they drove past the Dakota, which was not far from where they were staying, their driver pointed out the very spot where John Lennon had been assassinated back in 1980.

On that first day they were all a little in awe of the big, vibrant city. It was a place full of tall skyscrapers, big cars, and yellow taxis honking their horns. A city bursting with life, a city that never slept.

What a wonderful time they were all going to have.

The days passed quickly as they explored the city. Sometimes they went out en-masse, sometimes individually. They were such a close family that everyone felt comfortable talking about what *they* wanted to do, where *they* wanted to spend their precious time in this exciting place. Obviously, there were things they all wanted to do and places they all wanted to visit, so on those days Melissa hired the stretch limo and they travelled in style. On other days, they went out in small groups, preferring to use the subway or the bright yellow taxis. One day, they all went on the Staten Island ferry and then out to Ellis Island so they could see the magnificent Statue of Liberty at close quarters.

Some days they just roamed the streets, marvelling at the grid system that made it easy to navigate the area. Occasionally, they simply ventured from their apartments near West 81st Street right down to the Meatpacking District starting on West 14th Street.

Mind you, their limo driver had been very careful to point out all the dodgy places they should avoid as well as the highlights. Places like the Meatpacking District, which was once so thriving, was now in something of a decline, similar to much of the industrial waterfront area. It was a place full of rather seedy nightclubs and dubious-looking characters. They had a hard time believing that a once-thriving area had deteriorated so quickly, and found it equally difficult to imagine it ever being restored to a desirable space.

Daisy loved Harlem.

She especially loved the effect the place had on her family. She had never seen her dad and grandparents so happy.

It had been nearly 40 years since they left their hometown, and of course, many things had changed in that time. However, their family and friends hadn't changed one bit. The same people who had waved goodbye when they sailed off to England all those years ago were there to greet them at the docks on their arrival. There were hugs and tears, and Daisy could not believe how many relatives she had.

There were lots of incredibly attractive men, all as tall and as handsome as her dad and grandad. They all had impeccable manners, again like her father. As for the women, well, she had never seen so many beautiful, sassy women in one room before. The noise was deafening as everyone tried to talk at once.

"Hey Jeremy, man, how did you ever manage to get such a beautiful wife?"

She could see her dad puff up with pride when he heard this, and noticed how he pulled her mum towards him and smiled at her before replying.

"Well wouldn't you like to know, too bad you'll never find that out cos you're too lazy to leave Harlem!"

"Hey Sam, do you still play the sax or are you too old now?"

"Win, how have you ever managed to stay sane, living with that darn brother of mine?"

"Hey Daisy, come out the back with us and let's leave the oldies to talk."

Out the back, which proved to be a small square concrete yard, Daisy sat on a rickety old wooden chair while they fussed around her.

"Leroy, get a cushion for Daisy, those chairs ain't at all comfortable."

"Jerome, pour Daisy some of that lemonade."

"Turn that damn music down. We want to hear what our new cousin has to say."

"Joseph, stop looking all dreamy-eyed! Fetch Daisy a sweater, we don't want her catching her death from all these draughts."

Daisy looked around, at all her new-found relatives, people who, until now, had just been names or faces in photos. These photos had been popped inside Christmas cards with long letters accompanying them, relaying all the family gossip and information for the whole year. She had always loved it when the letters arrived at the house in Brixton. Nana Winifred would spread them out on the dining table, and while she read the letters out loud, Daisy's job was to try and identify all the different people mentioned.

THE SECOND DAISY

In a way, none of them were really strangers, even though she had never met them before.

In no time at all her shyness was gone, chased away by the warmth of the welcome she received.

The conversation veered from questions about her life in London to the pop scene there. Had she been to Ronnie Scott's jazz club? What was her favourite music? What were the latest fashions in London? What kind of cars did people drive? What was her job?

She was embarrassed to admit that right now, she didn't *actually* have a job, and that in fact, she hadn't *ever* had one, having gone straight from her unfinished college year to life as a pretend housewife while married to Henry.

None of them were shocked about her not having a job, but they were horrified to hear about her failed marriage.

"Oh gurl, you should have just walked out the first time he hit you."

"I can't believe he would cheat on a beautiful girl like you."

"Selfish, arrogant man. Gurl, you are so much better off without him."

"Yep, and now you have us; you don't need some white honky treating you bad."

By the second day, Daisy felt as though she had known her new relatives forever. While the older ones stayed at home catching up on all the family gossip, her cousins took her on walking tours of Harlem. As they roamed the streets people stared, unable to take their eyes off of the incredibly attractive and lively group.

None of them failed to notice how often Joseph tagged along. Joseph was a distant relative, a third cousin twice removed of her Nana Winfred. He was very tall, an amateur basketball player, a handsome gentle giant.

He always managed to plant himself right next to Daisy on these walks. At first she didn't notice, she was so busy taking in the sights and listening to the animated chatter of the others.

He didn't say much, just smiled a lot and listened carefully to every word she uttered.

"That boy Joseph has fallen hard, I reckon."
"What you talking about, girl?"

Winifred was standing in the kitchen of her sister Alice's apartment, helping her prepare the chicken. At Jeremy's insistence, they had eaten it almost every night since they arrived in Harlem.

"You dragged me away from here when I was just five years old, the least you can do is let me catch up on some of what I've been missing all these years."

Jeremy had always thought that his mum made the best fried chicken in the whole world, but now he was not so sure. His Aunty Alice's recipe was something else, he might dare to say it was even more delicious. But maybe that was just because he was eating it here, in this place, with these people.

Alice continued cooking as she spoke.

"I said that Joseph has fallen hard for your Daisy."
"But don't worry Win. He's a good boy. Good prospects, good manners. He won't mess her about like that husband of hers did."

"Well I don't blame the boy. Our Daisy is so lovely, such a good girl with a really big, loving heart, but I don't think she's ready for any romancing right now. Her heart is well and truly broken. I'm not real sure if she will ever mend properly. All the wind seems to have gone out of her sails and she ain't got no more sparkle."

Their Harlem visit was over far too soon.
Everyone was sad to say goodbye; it had been so wonderful to renew old relationships and to establish new ones. But alas, they were obliged to go to Alabama next. Tickets had been booked and plans made.

"I think we should leave Alabama a couple of days early and pop back here to say a proper goodbye to you all before we leave for England."
Melissa spoke as the matriarch of the group. After all, she had paid the majority of the expenses, so surely she was entitled to make such important decisions. She knew that the others, like her, would much rather spend time with the lovely people here in Harlem and in the rest of the city than with her snooty relatives at the plantation.

It was a long journey down to Melissa and Ruth's old home in Tuskegee, in Macon County, Alabama.

They travelled on a luxurious private bus crisscrossing the vast country, each of them desperate to see as much as they possibly could in the short time frame they had. Truth be told, they would all much rather have done a simple sightseeing trip to enjoy the new experiences the States had to offer, and not have to waste precious time visiting distant relatives in Alabama. In their hearts though, they all knew that both Melissa and Ruth needed to do it, to get closure from that part of their lives. The lives they lived on the plantation before they moved to England.

They stayed overnight, just to break up the long journey, in Shenandoah National Park at the Big Meadows Lodge. The lodge had been built in 1939 with stone hewn from the mountains. It was now listed on the National Register of Historic Places. It was nestled on a flat plain off Skyline Drive, with glorious views of the surrounding mountains, both the Blue Ridge and the Appalachians. They sat in the big wood-panelled lounge, sipping cocktails and listening to their fellow travellers' stories, including tales of hiking and encounters with black bears.

Afterwards, Daisy and Jeremy spent a few hours in the old library. It was raining hard outside, too hard to even contemplate going for a walk, and the others were all having a nap before dinner.

"Dad, look at all these old photos."

Daisy had found a book dating back to the 1920s, full of old photographs. It was called "Memories of the Mountains," and was filled with faded old snaps of another period of time, a time before computers, television, or air travel. These were photos of another world, here in the mountains.

Jeremy noticed that Daisy had gone quiet. He put down the book he was glancing through about early buildings in Birmingham, Alabama, and went to sit down beside her.

"Oh Dad, look at these kids all patiently queuing to choose a book from the mobile library."

He looked at the page she was pointing to and smiled. Trust his lovely girl to pick out such an evocative photo.

In the photo, a little mobile book cart was parked in front of a spectacular view of the mountains and half a dozen little barefoot children were standing politely in front of it, waiting their turn to remove a book from the dusty old wooden shelves. They ranged in age from about 12 or 13 years old down to the smallest, who was probably only 4 or 5. Their clothes were clean but raggedy, obviously handed down as each one outgrew them. The girls wore pinafore dresses made of rough cream-coloured calico and their long hair was plaited, tied up with an old piece of string. Still, the joy on their faces was obvious. The chance to borrow a book was obviously such a treat, for the travelling library probably didn't pass through their way all that often.

The two of them spent another half an hour together, father and daughter both curled up on the old sofa, looking at all the other photos in the book.

"I think my favourite is definitely this one," Jeremy chuckled as he pointed to one apparently taken in 1901 of a group of five men, obviously dressed in their Sunday best, posing outside a log cabin with a hand painted sign reading "WIVES WANTED."

"See Daisy, nothing has changed in more than a hundred years. Men still have to advertise for love!"

They were still laughing when Polly came down to remind her husband and daughter to get ready for dinner.

They were all glued to the bus windows for most of the road trip, soaking up the sights and marvelling at all the quaint little towns and large cities as they passed through. They stopped every few hours to stretch their legs and have some refreshments. Sometimes they would nod off, exhausted by the sheer monotony of the wide open spaces, with barely a tree or house in sight.

They all perked up as they hit the next township, excited at the thought of another authentic diner or glossy department store. They stopped at all of them, every Sears, Macy's, JCPenney, Dicks Sporting Goods, Barnes and Noble, and Walmart they could find. It seemed, or so they imagined, that the stock in these stores was so much more exciting than anything they could find in London, even in the big department stores. They all made so many purchases, far too many to fit into the bus's large luggage section, that they had to stop in a big town and visit a shipping company to arrange for everything to be sent back to England. Undeterred, they did pretty much the same in every place they visited. Someone just "had to have those two pairs of shoes or the cute little armchair."

Melissa smiled as she looked around the bus at her sleeping companions. Even Ruth, sitting beside her, had nodded off and was snoring gently.

Ruth, her very dearest friend and long-time companion. Ruth, who had taken care of her right from when she was a baby, the much-loved and cosseted youngest daughter of the plantation owner. The same plantation where Ruth's ancestors had been enslaved and treated so poorly.

She gently touched Ruth's hair. Everyone else loved her silver grey curls, touched with just a fleck of the original dark colour. But they made Melissa sad. Ruth was eleven years older than her, and the grey hair reminded her that one day, probably not too far from now, she would lose her beloved friend forever. The thought made tears well up into Melissa's faded blue eyes. Rather than wake Ruth up, since she knew she would wake up the minute she sensed there was anything wrong, Melissa turned her attention back to the book she was reading: *Perfume from Provence by the Honourable Lady Fortescue.*

She had bought the book from the Book Club at 121 Charing Cross Road in London back in 1946, just after the end of the second World War. She had read it many times since then, enchanted by the story of *"enlarging the little house we had bought—before the pound collapsed—in Provence."*

It had been years since she had last picked it up, but she had decided to bring it on this trip. She would read it first, then pass it on to the others in the family to enjoy. She knew that Flo and Vi, both being artistic, would love the illustrations, done so many years ago by someone called E.H. Shepard.

Although the book looked simple and inexpensive, Melissa knew it was special. It had been printed in austere times: *"The paper and binding of this book conform to the authorised economy standard. This edition 1946."*

Despite having been published almost 50 years ago, it seemed very modern:

> *Page 67: "If business is business in other parts of the world, here in Provence it is fun. Let those who complain of the snatch and grab methods of commerce in this century, and the rush and hustle of modern life, come and shop with me in a Provencal town."*

Melissa settled down in the comfort of her reclining bus seat and continued to read the exploits of Lady Fortescue. It was a good distraction for what was to come: her return to the place of her birth, a place that stood for so much she despised.

ALABAMA

"Will we be here to watch the harvesting? When exactly do they pick the cotton?" Daisy was a bit disappointed by her first sight of the cottonfields. She had read so many stories and listened to her Uncle Matty tell of the vast fields of fluffy white cotton, fields that stretched for miles and miles, further than the eye could see.

And now here she was, in Tuskegee, Alabama, at Melissa's old family home. All she could see as she stood on the edge of the fields were rows upon rows of green, spiky-looking plants, with not a ball of fluffy white cotton in sight.

Jeremiah, the farm manager, a handsome Black man in his late fifties and the son of Ruth's niece, smiled down at the pretty young woman standing next to him.

"Well, Miss Daisy, I reckon you've come just a month or so too early. We don't generally start harvesting till at least July. By that time, those bolls crack open and all the fluffy white cotton is exposed. That means it's ready for picking."

"Does it take long to pick it all? I remember my Aunty Ruth telling me how her brothers and sisters used to come in from the fields with bloody hands from where they had hurt themselves on all the sharp spikes of the plants. I always thought it seemed so cruel, sending little children out there all day in the hot sun. It used to make me cry when Aunty Ruth told me those stories. But I suppose it's better now. Now that there are mechanical pickers?"

Her voice trailed off. She had been so looking forward to coming here, to the plantation where Melissa and Ruth had grown up. Somehow though, now that she was here, she just felt sad.

The family in the big plantation house had all been quite welcoming of course, albeit in a rather subdued way. Melissa's eldest sister and her husband had inherited it after their parents died, and now it had been passed down to *their son,* Henry.

Daisy had been shocked when she first met him. Shocked by his appearance, by his resemblance to her Aunty Melissa, and even more by his manner, his arrogance. Shocked by the way he spoke to all the Black servants and by the dismissive way he glanced at Ruth, Samuel, Winifred, and Jeremy, the Black members of their family. Of course, he was nicer to her, but then again, *she wasn't as black as the rest of them, as her skin was more of a dark coffee colour.*

But, as Melissa reminded her, they were only here for a quick visit. It really didn't matter about the opinions of her family; they were people who had never left the safe confines of their luxurious, cosseted plantation lifestyle. Therefore, they understood nothing of the real world.

"Damn boll weevil, that's what wrecked the economy of this place. Now, more than half our land is turned to growing pine trees, peaches, and pecans.

And of course, once they brought in the mechanical pickers it led to the Great Migration. Most of our people, especially the young and fit men, went up North, leaving the fields to rot. Never gave a damn about leaving us all to cope with it. Just left, without a second thought for all we'd done for them."

Jeremy had read a lot about the cotton industry and was not in the least fazed by the arrogant man whose house they were in. It was truly a splendid old white plantation house, where they were all seated around a long, highly-polished wooden table, eating off fine bone china and drinking from expensive crystal glasses.

He greatly admired the style of the house, the Greek Revival Antebellum style of architecture, but he certainly did not admire the man who now owned it. In many ways he reminded Jeremy too much of another, rather arrogant young man, another Henry, Daisy's ex-husband.

"Actually Henry, I must disagree."

There was a stunned silence in the room and everyone looked at Jeremy, the man who had spoken.

"I beg your pardon?"

Their host looked as though he was about to have a seizure and his voice sounded strangulated, as though he was struggling to get the words out.

"What the hell do you disagree with?"

They all knew that what he really wanted to say was, "How dare you, an uppity Black man, stand in my house, eat at my table, and then have the audacity to argue with me?"

Daisy glanced around the room and noticed that everyone was suddenly sitting upright in their chairs, waiting for the response and unsure of exactly how this conversation was going to end. She smiled shyly at the two young Black maids and the rather handsome young Black waiter, all standing respectfully against the walls and waiting to clear the table ready for the next course.

Jeremy continued. "I think you will find Henry, that history tells a rather different story. I agree that the introduction of the mechanical pickers led to the Great Migration, but it gave those poor souls no choice. Most of them had lost their jobs, unemployment was rife, and the only way they could hope to support their families was by moving away. They mostly lived in pretty substandard housing, whole families often still trying to exist in the old slave quarters on the plantations. Many times, dogs were kept in better conditions."

Daisy recognised, by the tone of his voice, that her dad was about to lose it, to rant and rave about the unforgiveable effects that slavery had had on generations of people, *his* people.

Melissa spoke quietly, but authoritatively.

"As you know Jeremy, although I grew up in this house, I do not share the views of the rest of my family. However, we are guests tonight in Henry's home, so shall we just agree to disagree on this, and get on with enjoying our dinner? After all, we leave first thing in the morning, and I would like my final evening in my old family home to be a pleasant one. I have so enjoyed being reminded of the beautiful house and gardens where I married my beloved Theo."

And so it ended. Any discussion about the effects of slavery was over.

They were all staying in Melissa and Theo's old home on the estate. It wasn't the grand plantation house where she had grown up, but the much smaller Steamboat Gothic style house on the edge of the plantation. This was the house where the newly married couple had been so happy, where they had planned to raise a family and live happily ever after. Once Theo had died, dropping dead of a heart attack one sunny summer's day just a year after their wedding, Melissa's heart had broken into a thousand pieces, never to recover.

The little house had since been turned into an upmarket, rather exclusive guest house, so Melissa had booked out the whole place, insisting on paying the going rate, much to her nephew Henry's delight.

Having returned from the big house following the rather disastrous dinner party, they all sat on the covered porch, sipping brandy and reminiscing about their visit to Tuskegee and the surrounding places.

"I loved all the old buildings downtown, especially the old Macon County Courthouse, that old Butler Chapel Church, and all the old historical buildings down North Main Street. Glad to see that they've put protection orders on them, it would be tragic to see them pulled down."

"I was really interested to learn about the origins of the university, how it started out as the Tuskegee Normal School. How happy those early pupils would be to see that it is now recognised as a centre of excellence for African American education!"

"Did you read that bit in the Tuskegee News about the rising crime rates? Hardly surprising when unemployment here is so high."

"Did you know that Rosa Parks and Lionel Richie were both born here in Tuskegee?"

"I just wish we had been here when it was time to pick the cotton. But I guess you were right, Melissa, it would have been much too hot in July or August. Even now, in May, the days get pretty hot and uncomfortable."

Melissa and Ruth sat quietly, half listening to all the talk going on around them. They were both distracted, deep in their own thoughts and memories. Neither of them could quite believe the changes they saw in their hometown since their last visit in 1927. Obviously, the drop in cotton production had caused enormous upheaval. Where once there had been vast plantations, many of these had been sold off and turned into small farms with cattle, corn, and fruit as their main crops, rather than cotton.

"I couldn't believe it when Henry started talking about turning this whole place, the whole plantation, house and all, into a historic site, somewhere to hold weddings. I bet he'd even spruce up those old outbuildings where the slaves used to live and make them look fancy. Talk about white-washing history."

Melissa put down the glass she was drinking from and spoke quietly.

"Oh, Jeremy. I know you're cross with me for interrupting your conversation with Henry over dinner. I am sorry, but I could see where it was heading and I just didn't want a big row. Especially on my last night here. You know that I agree with you wholeheartedly, but I also know that even if you talked till you were blue in the face, you would never in a million years convince Henry or the rest of my stuck up family, that they were wrong. I spent the first nineteen years of my life arguing with them; it was only when I met Theo that I was finally able to speak my mind and be listened to."

She finished speaking and gazed across the fields. These were the same fields she had spent months gazing across after Theo died, hoping against hope that her handsome husband would come striding toward her. For a whole year, in those long ago and utterly miserable days, she had sat on this porch in this exact same spot, hoping and praying that it had all been a horrible dream, that Theo wasn't really gone.

None of them could say anything to bring him back or stop her from feeling heartbroken, so to change the subject and lighten the atmosphere, Flo spoke.

"What dreadfully dreary clothes those women were wearing tonight. All that money and absolutely no taste!"

They all burst out laughing. Trust Flo to bring fashion into the conversation!

FAREWELL TO HARLEM

They were all glad to get back to New York.

Somehow, knowing they only had a few days left to enjoy the city before their ship sailed back to England made them all super-charged. They got up early every day and ate a leisurely breakfast together in Melissa's suite. She had found a great chef—recommended by the owner of the apartments—who was happy to work for her on an ad hoc basis, preparing delicious meals whenever needed. The first morning he made pancakes with maple syrup and of course, everyone devoured them. His scrambled eggs and smoked salmon were legendary, and he even managed to cook a full English breakfast to everyone's satisfaction, down to producing eggs for Flo and Vi, "*sunny side up.*"

"Oh my, just wait till I get home and ask Joe to cook my eggs like that. He won't have a clue what I'm talking about! The only thing he knows how to cook is his ginger cake."

They all smiled. Throughout the entire trip, Flo had never missed an opportunity to bring Joe's name into the conversation. Her Joe, the love of her life and her husband for almost 70 years. A man she truly adored. A simple man with a big heart.

"I think you might be surprised just how much Dad knows about America, Mum." Vi spoke quietly, but they could all hear the amusement in her voice.

"What do you mean, love? Your dad's hardly ever set foot outside England. Well, apart from those couple of trips to France and Spain. But we had to drag him there, if you remember. He's a Londoner through and through, a real Cockney. He always says that home is best and he doesn't understand why people feel the need to go gadding off around the world."

"Oh Mum. Didn't you notice that book he's been reading for the last few weeks? I got it for him at one of the big bookshops on Oxford Street.

The Penguin Guide to New York City. It was only published a couple of years ago, so he's been brushing up on everything. He wants to impress you with all his knowledge when you get back from our trip. I can't believe you didn't notice him reading it; he's been glued to it since I got it for him."

Flo went quiet, suddenly feeling a bit guilty. She realised that she took so much for granted, always expecting Joe to be there for her, to pander to her every whim as he had done for so many years. He had always been so lovely, so supportive. All these years she had just taken his kindness for granted, she'd never stopped to think about what *he* wanted.

He had never really wanted her to open a dress shop. He would have been perfectly content just having a nice wife who cooked his meals, cleaned his house, and made him a few babies. She had been the one who always pushed him to do more, to have a life less ordinary. And now, to her eternal shame, she hadn't even noticed that he had been brushing up on his knowledge about New York so that he could have a decent conversation with her when she eventually got home.

They could all hear the emotion in her voice as she replied.

"Oh love, that was very kind of you. Did he ask you to get the book for him? That's so typical of my Joe. Always thinking about other people instead of himself. I bet he'll suddenly be a fount of knowledge. He'll probably drive me mad now, thinking he knows more than I do about New York! Oh I do hope he and Matty are all right. Maybe we shouldn't have left them all on their own so we could go gallivanting around the world like this."

And then she burst into tears, suddenly thinking about how much she loved her husband and how bereft she would be if anything happened to him.

Their last few days in New York passed in a whirlwind.

"Well I guess if my Joe is so keen to know everything, I'd better not let him down, right?"

Flo ignored her aching legs and the crippling pain from the arthritis in her hands, so determined was she to keep up with her absent husband and his encyclopaediacal knowledge of the city. She dragged them all to Chinatown, to Queens and the Bronx and Staten island. She made them go up to the top of the Empire State Building, marvelling at the views from the top and insisting that John take hundreds of photos with his new, fancy camera.

"Your dad will just love seeing all these snaps, John. Otherwise, he might not believe that we even went to these places."

John was happy to oblige. He wasn't sure if he had ever felt quite so complete before. Being on this trip with his whole family, a family from which he had chosen to be a little estranged for so many years due to his sexuality, was just wonderful. He realised now, having spent so much time in the last few weeks in their company, that he was just like them. He had spent so many years feeling different, inadequate because he didn't want what they all had, because he had never wanted a wife and children. Now he realised just how wrong he had been. They loved him for who he was. They didn't care one bit about whom he chose to love, they just loved him. And now they loved his Nigel too. How easily Nigel had slotted into their lives. This had been the most marvellous trip for them all. A real time of mending bridges, forging new bonds, restoring relationships, and realising that differences were good. Realizing that differences made everyone's lives more interesting and colourful.

"So, John, do you reckon we could squeeze in another quick trip to the Museum of Natural History today?'

Nigel had been fascinated by his first trip to the museum, just across the way from them on the Upper West Side. Working as a divorce lawyer for so many years had not given him much free time to explore his passions, but now that he was retired, he was determined to make time for his dreams.

"Of course. Does anyone else want to come with us? I thought we might find a nice little place to have a pizza for lunch afterwards?"

"I'm going to go for a long walk through Central Park. Some of my Harlem cousins are planning to come over and walk with me. You're all welcome to join us of course."

"Don't be silly Daisy. None of us could keep up with you lot. You walk so fast.

I couldn't even manage to keep up when we were doing that little Harlem walk the other day, you know, when I was showing you where I used to go to school and everything. Those young men are just too fit and fast for my liking. You youngsters go off on your own and have a good time. I know they'll take good care of you. And we'll see them all at the farewell dinner here on Friday."

Jeremy had only been going to school in Harlem for a couple of months when his parents announced they were moving to England. He was just five years old and had never known any other life. To him, his life in Harlem was perfect. Until he left, he had never known a life where all the people around him were a different colour, where he was treated like a second-class citizen. But as he grew up, he never regretted the move. He was only too aware that if he had stayed in Harlem he probably would never have fulfilled his dream of becoming an architect. And he certainly would never have met and married his Polly, or become a father to his darling Daisy.

"Well, I think I'd like to visit the SoHo district, just to see if it's like our SoHo in London. Does anyone fancy coming with me?"

They all smiled, knowing that Flo was just trying to get as much information as she possibly could to impress Joe. Woe betide that he might show her up by knowing more about New York than she did! Especially as all his knowledge was coming from a book!

They were all pretty emotional at the farewell dinner. Everyone was there, crowded into Melissa's apartment.

The chef, Bruno, was a flamboyant Italian gentleman of unknown age, whose height and girth were almost the same due to constant sampling of his own cooking. That night, he had served them a truly magnificent dinner of giant prawns served in cocktail glasses topped with shredded lettuce and a fancy dressing known as "Thousand Island." Then they had corn on the cob dripping with butter, and enormous grilled steaks topped with more prawns and apparently known as "Surf and Turf." For dessert he served pecan pie *and* key lime pie, both delicacies that none of the English contingent had ever heard of before. They were now in the enormous lounge area of the apartment, looking out over the twinkling lights of the city.

"I really wish we didn't have to leave tomorrow. This has been the most wonderful holiday ever."

They all nodded in agreement at Daisy's words.

"You're right Daisy, it has been wonderful. Thank you so much Melissa, for all your generosity. I don't think we'll ever be able to thank you enough; this trip has done us all the world of good."

Jeremy spoke for all of them. They were so delighted to see the change in their girl. As the weeks had worn on, some of her sparkle seemed to have returned. She obviously had such a wonderful time, and of course, she had thoroughly enjoyed spending so much time in the company of her young, friendly, and like-minded Harlem relatives.

"Actually Melissa, would it be all right if us young ones went next door to Mum and Dad's apartment? We'd quite like to play a bit of music and dance. I promise we won't make too much noise."

They all smiled as the young ones leapt out of their seats and rushed next door, ensuring they said polite goodbyes and words of thanks as they left.

"Well, I think we should put on a bit of music too. After all, it is our last night in New York, and I for one am still quite capable of moving about to a good beat!"

Within half an hour, all the older members of the family were strutting their stuff, even John and Nigel, who were usually very restrained. When it came time to bid farewell at midnight, they were all more than ready for their beds.

RETURN TO ENGLAND

Joe and Matty had been up since 6am. They didn't mind having to get up so early, as neither of them were great sleepers anyway. Their advancing years meant that they didn't need as much sleep as they had when they were energetic, fit young men, intent on taking the world by storm.

Today though, they were up early because they were excited. The family was coming home.

"Are you ready to pop next door for breakfast, Joe?"

"Yep, just give me a minute, Matty. I just want to give my hair a quick brush. Don't want Emma seeing me all messy."

The two old men, although missing their family terribly, had had a rather fun time for the last six weeks. They had watched whatever old rubbish they wanted on the television, sports and old detective movies, mostly. These were things on which neither of their wives were particularly keen. They had eaten every single meal next door at the Banana Box Café and now knew the little menu off by heart. In truth, they had eaten much better than they would have normally. At their age they sometimes didn't have much appetite, but somehow, being around the lovely Emma and her mum every day had sharpened their desires! They had also spent a few evenings in the pub at the corner of the street, rather enjoying being the centre of attention—two old relics from a past that now barely existed. They were well-known to lots of the young city workers who popped in for a quick drink on their way home, and generally all their drinks were bought for them, donated by their admiring audience!

"I'm going to miss coming here every day. Bet that old wife of mine won't let me. She'll just be worried I'm going to run off with you two lovely ladies!"

They all laughed. Despite his tough words, Joe was finding it hard to hide his excitement at seeing all the family again. He had missed them so much, especially his darling Flo and little Daisy. He just couldn't wait to give them both the biggest hugs.

They spilled out of the minibus, which was illegally parked in the cobbled street. Artillery Passage had been designed when the only form of transport was horse and carriage, so the narrow thoroughfare was certainly not wide enough to accommodate the bus or the copious amount of luggage that was being unloaded.

"Dad and I will stand here and sort this all out; you ladies just go inside and put the kettle on. I'm parched after that drive from Southampton."

Jeremy smiled at his dad. They would get the job done much faster without all the women fussing around, and anyway, he knew that Ruth and Flo couldn't wait to get inside to see the husbands they had missed so desperately.

"I think John and Nigel should be here any minute too. They can help us; they were just parking their car 'round the corner."

It had been such a wonderful trip that the other two men had been reluctant to leave the family and drive straight back to Nottingham as previously planned. Instead, they had decided to return to Artillery Passage for a few days to spend more time with them all.

By the time the four men unloaded all the luggage, dragged the heavy suitcases across the cobbles, and tipped the driver handsomely, the kettle had boiled, everyone was sitting around the old kitchen table, and Joe was cutting them all big chunks of his famous ginger cake.

They all seemed to be talking at once, each of them desperate to speak of their marvellous adventure.

"Now look here, you lot. It's wonderful to have you all back, but Matty and I have been having a fine old time in your absence and we'd quite forgotten how noisy you are! How about you all take it in turns to tell just one story each."

He was looking at Flo as he spoke, at the wife he had adored for all these years. He loved the way she looked so relaxed. He was always worried about her, nervous that she never gave herself much of a break, that she wore herself almost to death by always working and never complaining. But now, she looked wonderful. Younger somehow and very stylish, quite unlike the Flo who always wore rather simple, drab dresses so as not to outdo her clients.

"Looks like you might have spent a pretty penny or two on clothes, my girl. You're looking rather smart. That colour really suits you."

Flo blushed and tugged at the hem of the bright pink, Chanel-style suit she was wearing.

"Oh Joe, I did. There was just so much to choose from, I couldn't resist. I think I might have to take over that big wardrobe in the spare room just to house all my fancy new dresses."

Joe beamed. He didn't care if she filled the whole entire house with her new purchases, it was just so wonderful to have her back.

"Well Joe, I think you might have to open up that draughty old cellar as a storeroom. We all bought so much stuff. Not just clothes—although there are plenty of those—but we also got furniture, paintings, books, and a load of other things!"

"How on earth did you manage to fit furniture into your luggage?"

"Oh don't be silly, Dad. We couldn't bring it all back with us, so Melissa organised a big shipping container for everything and all our stuff will be arriving in a few weeks. Plenty of time for you to sort out the cellar before then!"

The rest of the day drifted by in a very pleasant haze of stories and laughter, punctuated with delicious food. Joe and Matty had arranged for some meals to be delivered from the café, so they all settled down to share vast bowls of spaghetti bolognaise, green salads, and scrumptious apple pie.

"Oh my, I had forgotten that simple food could taste so delicious. I loved all that fancy stuff we got on the ship, but I must say this is equally as good."

They all smiled at John as he spoke. John, the shy young man who had kept his life hidden from them for so many years, had changed. He was now much more comfortable in his own skin, more sure of his place in the world.

Flo was thrilled. It had always been such a sadness to her that John, her only living son, had chosen to spend almost all his adult life away from his family, worried that they might judge him.

She looked on happily, watching him interact with Nigel, the love of his life, and with Vi, his sister. They had all become very close on the trip and it made her happy to think that one day when she and Joe were gone, they would all be there for each other, a united family.

Daisy sat at the end of the long table in the same place she always insisted on sitting since she was a little girl. She studied each of her family members in turn as they spoke. Everyone had such stories to tell. Different stories, personal stories of their own experiences in America, wonderful, happy stories that would go down in family history.

Suddenly it was her turn, and she could feel all their eyes on her.

"Well, of course I loved it all. New York is such an exciting city—big, bright, and loud. I absolutely loved Harlem, especially getting to know everyone. It was such fun. And I loved all the shopping. And travelling in the bus, seeing all the little places. And the mountains. I was a bit disappointed I didn't see any cotton, though."

The stories went on well into the evening and finally it was time for Melissa, Matty, and Ruth to leave and return to their home in Bloomsbury. Everyone was sad to see them go; it had been an incredible trip and they all knew that such an adventure with the entire family was unlikely to ever happen again.

THE NEXT CHAPTER

A couple of months had passed since they returned from New York and already the memories of the trip were slightly fading.

John and Nigel ended up staying on for another two weeks, reluctant to drag themselves away from the bosom of their family. The night before they left, they took Joe, Flo, and Vi to the pub on the corner—the old pub where Joe used to go for a pint with his mates from the docks each Friday night when they got paid. Now the old place was unrecognisable, with flowery wallpaper, upholstered chairs, and shiny marble surfaces.

"Actually Mum and Dad, we have some news." John smiled at Joe and Flo as he spoke.

"Nigel and I have decided to move down to London. It seems silly to be stuck up in Nottingham on our own when all the people we love most in the world are here. We've found a nice apartment in the same block where Melissa, Ruth, and Matty live, a basement one with a bit of a garden. We've decided to sell the old farmhouse and downsize."

Flo burst into tears and Joe smiled gratefully at his son. This would mean the world to them both now that they were getting on a bit in age, to have their boy nearby. Not to mention, it would take the pressure off Vi a little. She was still working in the West End department store, and they knew she always felt a bit guilty leaving her aging parents home alone.

It hadn't taken them long to sell the farmhouse. It was a beautiful home, one they had put all their energy and funds into making spectacular. The first people to view it had insisted on offering the full asking price plus a large additional sum for all the furniture and artwork that wouldn't fit into their new place.

At first, John had been upset at the thought of leaving behind so many of the treasures they had collected over the years.

"Come on John, it's just stuff. We can't take it with us when we die, so what's the point of hanging onto it all now? We'd just be dragging it around the country, or worse, dumping it all into a storage unit. We bought it for this house and it fits perfectly here, let's just let the new owners enjoy it all. And anyway, think of all those fabulous antique shops we can explore on the King's Road. I bet we'll have the new place stuffed to the brim in no time."

Just four months later it was done. The farmhouse in Nottingham was sold and John and Nigel were happily nestled in their new mansion flat. Their life was suddenly easier, happier, and much more fulfilling than it had ever been. They made new friends, went out to dinner most nights, and met up with all the family in Artillery Passage every Sunday for a big roast lunch.

Daisy had spent the last couple of months helping at the architectural firm. It had been lovely spending so much time with her family but she was beginning to get itchy feet, desperate to start a life of her own. It was good being back home, of course, good to be in the familiar space she had known all her life. It had all been such a comfort to her at first, a great place to curl up and lick her wounds. Now, though, maybe it was time to move on?

"Mum, what would you think about me looking for a job?"

The thought terrified her. She had never had a proper job, hadn't even finished her college course thanks to her relationship with Henry.

"Oh love, I think that's a great idea. Your dad and grandad would miss you terribly of course; they say you're the best assistant they've ever had. Apparently, you're a real whiz with the filing cabinet."

"Well I did see a sign in a bookshop, you know that big one on Tottenham Court Road? They were advertising for an assistant in their little lending library. You don't need to sell anything, just keep the books tidy and help people if they need anything."

"Oh love, that sounds perfect for you. I bet they would be very interested in you, with your experience studying literature at college."

"But won't they ask difficult questions about why I gave it up and why at my age, I've never had a proper job?"

Polly looked down at her beautiful daughter.

"Oh my love, anyone would be happy to have you. You are young, intelligent, and determined. If you get an interview, just be honest with them. Tell them you married young, but are now divorced and ready to start your life anew."

That was that. Daisy took her mum's advice. She applied for the job, had an interview, and was offered the position on the spot.

It turned out to be the best possible thing she could have done. The job at the bookshop combined all the things she was best at: reading, organising, and mixing with like-minded people. She made new friends and started socialising again. Her sparkle came back.

Six months had passed since Daisy began working in the bookshop, and she was now in sole charge of the lending library. It was situated right at the back of the vast store, tucked out of sight and unknown to the casual shopper.

There were thousands of books in the small space, all jostling for their place on the old wooden shelves. Some of them were ancient, original stock from when the space had been set up back in the late 30s.

It had been the brainchild of the shop owner's daughter, a feisty young woman called Felicity Featherstone. She had seen a gap in the market, realised that not everyone could afford to buy brand-new books, and persuaded her father to let her use a small spot at the back of his shop to try her idea. It had been an instant success. Lots of working-class people who were

THE SECOND DAISY

unable to afford such luxuries on their sparse incomes were delighted to borrow books for just a penny. Young women on their way home to the slums from their jobs "up West" would pop in to pick up the latest romance novel, and working men would be delighted to find a detective or cowboy book on the shelves. Initially, all the books came from the main shop. They were books that didn't sell well, or weren't very popular with the paying clientele, but over the years the stock had expanded to include second-hand books that had been bought at full price and then donated.

By the time Daisy started working there in the 1990s, the place had become an institution. Everyone had heard of the old penny library. One of the first things Daisy did was to find an old sepia photo of Felicity Featherstone and have it framed, at her own expense, in an old Art Deco wooden frame that suited it perfectly. She had no idea whether the old woman was still alive; the shop had long ago been sold out to a large consortium and was now just one in a faceless chain of such stores. However, the lending portion of the shop had been allowed to remain in place. It had become something of a tourist attraction, listed in all the guide books alongside the likes of Madame Tussauds and the Tower of London.

Some days it was crowded with people just being curious, snapping away with their cameras. Daisy was always happy to tell them the story of how it began, how it had changed the lives of many ordinary people.

On one particular sunny afternoon in June, she had just finished telling a group of Japanese tourists the shop's history when she noticed an older woman staring intently at the photo

165

of Felicity on the wall. There were tears in her eyes as she turned her old, wrinkled, but still rather beautiful face, towards Daisy.

"Thank you, my dear. You have made an old lady very happy today. You see, that's me in this photo, when I was just a young woman with the world at my feet."

Daisy was stunned. She had never imagined that Felicity Featherstone was still alive, but now she could see the resemblance to the pretty young woman in the photo. The library was almost empty save for a couple of regulars, people Daisy knew just popped in every afternoon for a warm and comfortable place to sit and read.

"Oh Felicity, that's wonderful. I am so happy to meet you. Have you got time to stay and have a cup of tea with me? I would so love to hear all about your life."

Felicity wiped away her tears and smiled.

"My dear child, I have all the time in the world these days. I would be delighted to drink tea with you."

And so it began. A friendship between two women, one near the end of her life, the other just searching for a new start to hers.

Felicity's story was fascinating to Daisy. She couldn't believe how many similarities there were between her life and the life of the older woman.

Like her, Felicity had been an only child. Her mother had died when she was born and her father adored her. The only problem in his mind was that she was just a girl. *Just a girl.* Not a son onto whom he could pass his wealth. He was a fairly modern man and he loved his daughter very much, but the times were different. There was no way he would consider leaving his wealth, his vast property empire, or his bookshop—the biggest and best bookshop in London—to a mere *girl*. Obviously she would marry one day and then, if the chap was suitable, he might consider signing it all over, confident in the knowledge that his girl would be financially looked after by her husband.

The problem was, Felicity never married. She had had two proposals from chinless wonders who just wanted to inherit her father's wealth, but she had refused them both. She was unwilling to give up her freedom to such dismal specimens of manhood. There had been a man once, a man she had fallen head over heels in love with, but he was a penniless artist and her father had sent him packing. A year or so after that sad affair she had come up with the idea of the lending library, and in an effort to cheer her up, her father had reluctantly agreed.

"Like you do now Daisy, I used to spend every waking hour in this place. There was a little flat above the shop, and I persuaded my father to let me move into it. I had to take my maid, Phoebe, with me; he would never have allowed me to live alone back then. In the 1930s, such a thing would have been unthinkable. We had such fun, Phoebe and I. She was my very best friend in the whole world. After this place was sold to that horrible chain of companies, we had to move out of the flat, so I bought a little place in Chelsea for us. They wouldn't let me stay working here, said I was too old-fashioned and that the place needed modernising. I haven't been back here for years, couldn't bear to come near this place because it upset me too much. But I lost Phoebe a few months ago—she had a bad stroke and never recovered. So now that I'm all alone, I thought I'd just pop in for one last look at the old place before I die."

"Oh Miss Featherstone, what a story you have. I am SO glad you came back. I think we have a lot in common. Could you come again tomorrow and tell me some more?"

The days turned into weeks and the weeks into months, and Felicity Featherstone popped into the little library at least twice a week. She rolled up her sleeves and helped Daisy rearrange all the bookshelves, showing her how the place had looked when it first opened. The place took on a new lease of life. It was no longer just a tatty little library; it became a historical goldmine. Books were unearthed that had probably not seen daylight since the 40s. Rare first editions were discovered and the two women established a place of such efficiency and order that regulars shook their heads, uncertain if they approved of such changes.

"History of Shoreditch and Spitalfields books are in aisle S, row 16, Mr. Smith."

"I think we have a few old Regency romances in aisle F, probably row 3 or 4."

"We're having another clear out of the old stockroom tomorrow, Janice, so do pop back in on Saturday! I'm sure you'll find something you like."

There were a few raised eyebrows from the rather snooty store manager, but once he learnt the identity of the old lady, he was thrilled. Another drawcard for the shop, another reason for people to come to *his* store rather than that fancy one on Oxford Street. He contacted the local paper and they loved the story. Photographs were taken, and for a few weeks Felicity was a local celebrity. Hundreds of people poured into the shop, eager to see that such an icon had returned.

Things settled down after a while, of course. Felicity became old news, just another story wrapped around someone's fish and chips. At the same time, a deep bond had been formed between her and Daisy, and she became a big part of the young woman's new life. Daisy visited her at her beautifully elegant furnished flat in Chelsea, and Felicity went to Artillery Passage for one of Flo's famous Sunday roasts. Everyone loved her of course, and in no time at all she was almost part of the family, another addition to their very mixed but loving bunch.

"I was thinking, Daisy, you're a bit wasted here. You've done a marvellous job getting the old place back to its former glory, but you're much too young and beautiful to be wasting your whole life just sitting around this place."

"Oh Miss Featherstone, I love it here. Whatever else would I do? I'm not qualified for much else. I'm not qualified for anything at all, actually."

The older woman heard the sound of slight despair in Daisy's voice and her heart broke for the girl. By now she had heard all the stories of Daisy's ill-advised marriage, as well as her divorce, and it had made her so sad. Another young woman—just like she had been once upon a time—who had not been able to fulfill her potential because of a man.

"Actually Daisy, I think you could conquer the world if you tried. Please don't let one small setback stop you from living your life. I know how scary it is to step out of your comfort zone and into the unknown, but believe me, you must try. You never know what's out there till you go and look for it."

Felicity Featherstone died just three weeks after giving Daisy that advice.

Six weeks after her funeral, Daisy left the little lending library for good, carrying a cardboard box that held inside it a few old books and the framed photo of her friend.

She had given up her job at the bookshop to do as she had been told. She was going off to find her passion.

AN UNEXPECTED THING

Flo stood in the cobbled street and looked across at the shop window.

Her shop.

For a long time, she wept.

It wasn't her shop any longer, but that wasn't why she was so emotional.

She wept because she was remembering that day, so, so long ago, back in the 1920s.

The day when she had first opened her little dress shop in Artillery Passage.

The day her own mum, the first Daisy, stood in this exact same spot and wept because Flo had called her shop "POLLY'S" after Daisy's beloved mother.

Polly had been born in the Workhouse and had died when the first Daisy was just three years old. The sight of her mum's name in big gold letters, etched onto the little shop window, had been the reason Daisy cried that day in 1925.

Now, more than 70 years later, Flo found herself crying for almost exactly the same reason.

The little shop window looked splendid, almost exactly the same as it had when the house was built back in the 1700s. The only difference now was that the old glass in the bow-fronted window had been replaced. Some kids had run amuck, throwing stones into every shop window on the old street, and a stone had cracked one of the ancient panes. The family found some old recycled Victorian glass in a scrapyard and replaced the broken piece. Now, no-one but an absolute purist would be able to tell the difference.

Etched on the new pane of glass in large gold letters were the words

"DAISY'S BOOKSHOP."

Joe put his arm around his wife and held her tightly while she sobbed.

"Oh Joe, just think how proud my mum would be if she were alive to see this."

Joe smiled. He knew how much Flo still missed her mum, even though she had been gone for 26 years.

"You're right, love. Your mum would have been so thrilled to see your little shop still in use, even more thrilled to see how well our Daisy is doing after everything she's been through."

Daisy stood inside the crowded little bookshop and looked around. All the people she loved most in the world were here. Her family gazed lovingly at her, and even Eli and

Emily had ventured out of Hastings to come up to London for the occasion. Emily was looking particularly splendid tonight in a lime green, full-length dress covered in large white daisies. Eli also looked remarkably different, spruced up in a rather sharp bottle-green suit of indeterminate age.

Tonight Daisy was wearing her new dress, a stunning creation made of velvet that showed off her slim figure. She had been a bit worried that it was too tight, but her mum and Flo had assured her it was perfect. The olive green colour of the fabric matched her eyes, and with her dark brown curls tumbling loosely around her beautiful face, she rather resembled a mermaid.

Huge bowls full of large white daisy flowers were dotted around the room, a tribute sent via Interflora from her American family.

She tapped a spoon lightly on the crystal glass she was holding, terrified she would break it if she hit it too hard. She had borrowed the set of glasses from her Aunty Melissa, and although she knew her aunt wouldn't care if some of them got broken in all the excitement, they were precious to *her, a part of her childhood*. She had such fond memories of being allowed to use them as a very young girl, from which she was allowed to drink her orange squash. Now, here she was, all grown up and using them to drink champagne, toasting the success of her very own little shop.

DAISY'S BOOKSHOP.

The idea had come to her when they were in New York. She had been roaming the streets, dragging her Dad around with her. In Greenwich Village they had come across a quirky little bookshop.

The father-daughter pair had gone inside; her dad wanted to search for old architecture books and she just enjoyed soaking up the atmosphere. Jeremy got into conversation with the owner and Daisy could hear the murmur of their voices in the background. As she tuned in, she could hear her dad telling the tale of how he, the boy from Harlem, had gone to England at the age of five, and how, despite all the odds, he was now an architect running his own business.

She loved hearing him tell his life story. He was a natural storyteller and of course, he had a tale worth telling. In fact, thinking about it, she realised that most of her family and certainly some of her friends, like old Eli and Emily from Hastings, all had tales that were worth telling—and hearing. But of course, they would never get 'round to writing their own stories down, they would die and their stories would die with them. This thought made Daisy so sad; she realised that perhaps, she should record their stories for them. They could serve as a legacy for the future generations. Maybe writing other people's life stories was her calling. Although she didn't have much of a life of her own at the moment, perhaps she could write about the lives of other people. Maybe writing was her passion, just like sewing had been for GG Flo?

The Greenwich Village bookshop was tiny, wedged between a barber's shop and a deli. To Daisy, though, it was an emporium, a magical place full of delights.

She and Jeremy left several hours later, both laden down with several purchases and thrilled with their new acquisitions.

But for Daisy there had been something else. An awakening. A realisation that despite her divorce and all the misery it entailed, she still had a bright future to look forward to. There, in the hustle and bustle of New York City, she thought about how she had always loved reading, along with bookshops and libraries. She thought about how, during her short marriage to Henry, she spent so many hours at the local library trying to bury her sadness in all the books. She thought too about her afternoons spent reading to the elderly men at Old Frederick Palmer's mansion. That day, she felt her spirits rise and her heart gladden.

Once they were back in London, she had taken the job at the little lending library and met Felicity Featherstone. That short time in her life had changed everything; it steered her in another entirely different direction and brought her to where she was standing now. She glanced at the framed sepia photo of her friend, hanging in its beautiful Art Deco frame on the wall opposite.

"Thank you all so much for coming."
Her voice shook slightly as she spoke.

"I never imagined that one day I would own my very own bookshop. This is such a dream come true for me, and I could never, ever, have done it without you all. Thank you all so very much."

She paused to catch her breath before continuing.

"Firstly, I have to thank my wonderful GG Flo for allowing me to use her dress shop. This place has been her life for nearly 70 years and I am very honoured that she is entrusting me to look after it for her. And of course, I get to live here with her and my Great Granddad Joe, for free!"

They all laughed. Everyone knew it was a win-win situation for everyone involved.

Daisy had been able to set up the little bookshop on the ground floor, right on the cobbled street where Flo's dress shop had been. This meant that she would live in the big house with them and Grandma Vi, and so would be on hand to help whenever she was needed. Hopefully, this would mean that when the time came, Flo and Joe could die in their own bed, in the house they had shared for the entire seven decades of their married life.

"Of course, the rest of my family have been absolutely wonderful, too. You have all supported me so much, constantly encouraging me and helping me to plan everything and get organised. It helps having two architects in the family!"

She glanced at Jeremy and Samuel as she said this and they both beamed. They were both so very proud of their little girl.

"Mum, Nana Winifred, Grandma Vi, Ruth, Aunty Penny, and Aunty Melissa, you have all been so fantastic, assisting me in so many ways. I could never have made it look this good without all your wonderful ideas."

"And Uncle Matty," she smiled at the old Black man sitting in the weathered leather armchair.

"Thank you for everything. You have been one of my greatest inspirations and we have had such fun together, collecting all the photos and press cuttings from the 1920s."

The little bookshop was a very eclectic place filled with comfy furniture and beautiful oak shelves loaded with books of every genre. Each wall was filled with photographs and memorabilia of times long since passed.

"But my biggest thanks must go to my namesake, the original Daisy, my great-great grandmother. Her early life was very hard; she didn't have a mum or dad around and she didn't even learn to read until she was grown. I have to think that she would be very proud of what we, her family, have achieved."

"Please raise your glass to the first Daisy."

Daisy's Bookshop quickly became a roaring success. It was such a warm and inviting place. People often dropped in just to buy one book, then ended up staying for hours.

There was a coffee machine permanently on the go and one corner of the old wooden counter was stacked high with delicious cakes and savouries under big glass domes. All the food was sourced from Emma and her mum's Banana Box Café. The two women had proved to be such a great support to Joe and Matty while the others had been away on their American jaunt. In fact, they had been looked after so well that both men had put on several pounds in weight during the rest of the family's absence.

Apart from the coffee, there was tea available of every possible kind: English Breakfast, Earl Grey, Lapsang Souchong, Peppermint, Green, Black, Chamomile, and Rooibos. If none of that suited their fancy, customers could just have some hot water with a slice of lemon or a sprig of mint. Everything was served in beautiful bone china tea cups and saucers.

Many of these had come from Old Frederick's mansion in Marylebone, the rest came from Flo's china cabinet.

Visitors lounged on comfy old armchairs and sofas, and small children sprawled on the floor using brightly-coloured beanbags.

The original dress shop had been extended and now the whole ground floor had become a space to sell books. There were several small rooms off the hallway, each decorated in the same slightly eclectic manner with lots of additional nooks and crannies to get tucked up in with a good book.

Some of the sofas had beautifully-patterned throws slung across them, and there were cushions covered in bright sari silks stacked up on the wooden window seats. Aunty Penny had sent these from India as a shop-warming gift.

Looking at the silks made Daisy smile as she remembered another glorious trip.

That time, many years ago—before she ever married Henry—when she, Polly, Grandma Vi, GG Flo, Aunty Melissa, Ruth, and Nana Winifred had all gone to visit Aunty Penny in India. She had been living there for many years, since she left London as a shy 19-year-old. They had all assumed she lived simply, so they were quite overwhelmed when they arrived at her house. It was an old converted palace that tripled up as her home, factory, and the sanctuary for twenty young Indian girls whom she had rescued from the streets and trained to become excellent seamstresses.

The family had an incredible time taking in all the local sights, visiting the Taj Mahal and other beautiful palaces, and getting to know all the touching stories of the young girls now in Penny's care.

"Well, you certainly did manage to find your passion, Penny, even though you had to leave us and move halfway across the world to do it."

Vi had spoken with a catch in her voice. Of course she had always tried to love her girls equally, but Penny had been born at a very difficult time in her life. She had suffered badly from the Baby Blues, and Penny had been such a quiet little girl—so different from Polly. It had been so difficult to know if she was ever truly happy.

She looked across at her two daughters, as well as her granddaughter, squinting her eyes to block out the bright Indian sun. How she loved them all. It made her heart sing to see the three of them together, enjoying each other's company.

"Mum, come over here, help us choose some nice fabrics to take back for stock for GG's shop. Oh, and maybe a length or two for ourselves to run up a few dresses!"

"How Old Frederick would have loved all this. Do you remember all the lovely Indian and Chinese drapes, cushions, and carpets he had at the mansion? He would have been so proud to see how well our Penny was doing."

At the conclusion of their trip to India they ended up having to ship three huge crates of fabric back to London. There were yards and yards of beautiful, jewel-coloured silks. None of the women could resist them.

Daisy smiled to herself now, remembering the glorious time.

Brought back to the present moment, Daisy saw that the sari-covered cushions looked beautiful in the London bookshop, especially on the darkest of winter days. In glorious shades of cerise pink, tangerine orange, lime green, and turquoise blue, they somehow seemed to cheer the place up, to bring a bit of the exotic Indian continent right to the middle of the East End. Every time Daisy looked at them she smiled. As she got older, she realised just how important it was to keep creating memories like that with the people she loved, because one day, those people would be gone and memories were all she would have left of them.

She was thrilled with her new space and spent many, many happy days working long into the night to ensure that all the books were back in their rightful places, ready for the next morning's crowd.

Sometimes she would just lean against the old wooden counter that had seen so much life, close her eyes, and grin, knowing that she had created a very special place indeed—a place that people of all kinds loved to visit.

Each day was different. After all, it wasn't just an ordinary book shop. It was like several old history books had come to life.

The house itself was an architectural gem, with almost all the original features still in place.

Daisy had been very careful to represent every branch of her family tree in the bookshop. Rather than mixing everything up with no real thought to each section, she had made designated areas.

In one room, she had hung photos of the shop that were taken in the 1920s when Flo and Jo had first moved into Artillery Passage. From the outside the place looked exactly the same now, except for the name etched in gold lettering.

Some of Flo's original creations—dresses she had designed in the 30s—were hung in specially-made glass frames on the walls. Pride of place was given to the first dress she had ever sewn, the one that started her on her life's journey. It was a stunning gown made of scraps of satin, a muddle of colours stitched lengthwise so the pieces of fabric hung like petals. It was Flo's pride and joy and had hung in her shop window, whatever the current fashions, for more than 60 years.

Flo had cried when Daisy first showed her this room. She was overcome with emotion for her memories and for her hopes and dreams as a young woman, but mostly because her great granddaughter had taken such care to honour her life. She had been younger than Daisy was now when she opened her dress shop, and although she was sad to see it go, she realised that now it would exist forever, etched into people's experiences of this new space. The tears had poured down her old wrinkled face as Daisy held her arm and marched her around the little room, pointing out all the small details that Flo might have otherwise missed. She showed her the collection of wooden cotton reels, some with brightly coloured thread still attached and all piled up in a big basket on the old wooden table. Flo noticed it was the very same table that she had used as a cutting table all those years ago, now with stacks of books hiding the marks and gouges where her scissors had sometimes slipped. She stroked the tabletop, feeling the familiar pleasure, but was then dragged away by Daisy to look at the shelves covered in some old fabrics that were secured in place with Flo's old wooden measuring tapes. A little wicker basket stood alongside them, and she remembered clearly the day—back in 1921—when she was just 14 years old and Old Frederick Palmer had bought it for her in the little haberdasher's shop in Marylebone High Street.

In another spot, Daisy had hung all the old photos of the docks.

This quickly became the favourite spot for Great-Grandad Joe to hang out; he would regale any willing listeners with tales of his exploits as a young docker. Generations of his family had worked on the docks, mostly on the south side of the River Thames near his childhood home in the Peabody Buildings of Southwark. To his surprise, Joe had found the camaraderie of working at St. Katharine's Docks to be just as good as what he was used to south of the river, at Surrey Commercial Docks. While he was still employed at the Docks, he had become very involved with the local trade union movement, fighting for better working conditions and pay for all the men. It had never occurred to any of them that one day the docks would close, the need for them gone. Generations of his family had worked on the river, and it was sad to think that none of the young men to come ever would. It had been backbreaking work, but honest work, and he missed it.

He would have happily spent his remaining years there, working hard all day to lift heavy crates full of bananas, tea, sugar, and other such things. He had loved his work, loved the camaraderie of his friends and workmates, and had always looked forward to drowning his sorrows every Friday night at one of the old pubs lining the dockside. But when he met his Flo, he was lost. Lost to his own hopes and dreams, instead happily focusing on hers. When she had suggested moving to Spitalfields and opening her own dress shop, he had been horrified at the thought of leaving his beloved Southwark and to think about living north of the river. He was also horrified at the thought of the responsibilities that come with a wife, family, and business. But Flo and Old Frederick Palmer had already hatched their plan.

All in all, it was a decision he had never regretted. He and Flo had been so very happy together. He had adored her for more than 70 years now, that magnificent young woman he had married on Christmas Eve in 1924, and she adored him right back. Still though, having this little exhibition of the docks in the bookshop filled a great gap in his life. He could wander in whenever he liked to gaze at the old photos and relive the wonderful memories in his head.

All around the walls of the bookshop were family portraits. There was one of the first Daisy as a little girl, circa 1889, in a long, Victorian frock with a straw bonnet on her head. Another with Daisy alongside her husband Blackie, and his horse and cart full of sacks of coal. There was Old Frederick and Young Fred outside their Brighton townhouse, posing beside their much-loved car—a cream-coloured 1920s Rolls-Royce Silver Ghost.

There were numerous old sepia photos and Daisy could name everyone in them; she had spent so many happy hours as a child rifling through them, fetching them one by one out of the old tin box. Now, here they all were, enlarged in fine gold frames to match the lettering on the shop window. All her ancestors were present in her little shop—even the ones she had never been able to meet.

There were lots of other photos and paintings too, of places and people who all had some kind of connection to her beautiful family.

There was a wonderful old oil painting of a very young Melissa with her handsome husband Theo, as well as a youthful-looking Ruth and Matty.

That one was based on a photo that had been taken outside their little house in Alabama in 1920, just a few months before Theo had died.

Once they were finally settled in Bloomsbury, Melissa had commissioned one of their new painter friends—a chap called Duncan Grant—to make an oil painting using the original photo as his guide.

There were also paintings of the cotton fields of Alabama and photos of big white plantation houses, sitting alongside pen and ink sketches of the old slave quarters. The pictures hung together on the walls, cheek by jowl, much closer than their subjects had ever been allowed to be in real life.

Photos of Harlem, old ones from the 20s, hung alongside the more modern ones snapped by Grandpa Samuel from their most recent trip. Daisy especially loved the one where they made him pose outside Minton's Playhouse, the club where as a young man, he had worked as a cleaner. She adored the modern photo of Nana Winifred outside the Apollo Theatre, the place where the young pair had met all those years ago.

"Your nana was the finest thing I had ever laid my eyes on. You should have seen her, Daisy, my girl. She was so mighty fine, bossing us all about, standing there all uppity in her tight little pink dress."

It made Daisy smile every time she looked at her family history hanging on the walls. Her grandparents were obviously still so much in love, even after all these years. So were her parents. She sighed, and even through the happiness felt a familiar sadness creeping in. Would she ever find a love like that?

A love that all the women in her family seemed to have found at least once—a man who loved and adored them, and worshipped the very ground they walked on.

She closed her eyes tightly to try and stop the tears that were threatening. She allowed herself to wallow for a few minutes before opening them again, then continued to look at the rest of the pictures on the walls of a family made up of pure love and respect.

She thought about the words Grandma Vi had said at dinner that first night of their trip on the QE2, when they were on their way to New York.

Vi rarely said anything much, so when she did speak, it was usually worth hearing.

"They say that blood is thicker than water, but I don't think that's necessarily true in our family. Just look at us all."

It was true that they were a very unusual group, a family bonded together by chance, love, and respect. Daisy had a family that she would never want to change, even if someone offered her all the riches in the world.

She stopped in front of the portrait of the first Daisy, taken on her wedding day in 1905—the day she had married Blackie.

That Daisy had had such a different life. She was born into poverty, orphaned at just three years old, and unable to read or write until she was grown. How happy and proud she would have been to see her great-great-granddaughter, her namesake, the second Daisy, fulfilling her dreams and owning her very own bookshop.

She stroked the faces gently through the glass: the great-great-grandparents she loved, even though she had never been lucky enough to know them.

What a wonderful legacy they and all the others in her family were leaving.

A true blended family, a mix of colour, class, and background; a family of equals, regardless of their start in life.

Suddenly, Daisy was startled by a gentle tapping on the shop window. It was too early for any customers; the shop didn't open until nine-thirty and it was only just a little after eight o'clock. She looked up and through the old glass window she saw a face. It was a face she saw often these days, a face she was beginning to love.

He seemed to pop into the shop almost every day on one pretext or another. She opened the door and hugged him.

"Hello, Joseph."

The tall young basketball player from Harlem was standing in front of her. The man who had followed her halfway across the world. Just maybe, he was her future. Maybe together, they would write the next chapter of her family's saga?

THE END

REFERENCES

The Old Curiosity Shop, a novel by Charles Dickens
(Published 1840)

The Pillars of the Earth, a novel by Ken Follett
(Published 1989)

Perfume from Provence, a novel by The Honourable Lady Fortescue
(Quoted from an edition published in 1946, book originally published in 1935)

Did you enjoy this book?
Please leave me a review!
Your feedback is important to me; please leave a review wherever you purchased this book, or meet me on my website: www.patbackley.com
I look forward to hearing from you!

AUTHOR BIOGRAPHY

Pat Backley is an English woman who, at the age of 59, decided to become a Kiwi.

She now lives in New Zealand. When not writing, she loves to travel the world and catch up with all her friends (COVID permitting). She particularly enjoys spending lots of time in Fiji with her beloved extended Fijian family.

She also gardens, paints, reads, and loves activities like interior design, walks on the beach, and socialising. In short, she lives an ideal existence, but it wasn't always this easy. More on that in her recently published memoirs: *FROM THERE TO HERE, WITH AN AWFUL LOT IN BETWEEN.*

This book: *THE SECOND DAISY* is a sequel to Pat's first novel *DAISY,* which was published in 2020.

In 2021 she also co-authored a coffee table book: *THE WARRIOR WOMEN PROJECT A Sisterhood of Immigrant Women.*

www.ingramcontent.com/pod-product-compliance
Lightning Source LLC
Chambersburg PA
CBHW031247290426
44109CB00012B/466